LOST CHURCHES AND CHAPELS OF HULL

Compiled by

David Neave

with contributions from
**Geoff Bell, Chris Ketchell
and Susan Neave**

**Hull City Museums & Art Galleries
and the Hutton Press**

1991

Published by Hull City Museums & Art Galleries

and the Hutton Press Ltd.
130 Canada Drive, Cherry Burton, Beverley
North Humberside HU17 7SB

Typeset and printed by
Image Colourprint Ltd.,
Anlaby, Hull.

ISBN 1 872167 29 2

ACKNOWLEDGEMENTS

For much of the information in this booklet we are
greatly indebted to those who have preceded us in the
study of Hull's churches and chapels. We have drawn
freely upon Bernard W. Blanchard's pioneering thesis on
'Nonconformist Churches in the Hull District', 1955, and
the writings of Edward Ingram, in particular his entries
on Anglican churches, and those of Keith Allison on
other places of worship, in the *Victoria County History,
East Riding*, vol. 1, 1969. Additional information on
Methodist chapels comes from R. F. Drewery's unpublished 'History of Methodism in Hull', 1974. David
Woodhouse generously provided photographs and text
concerning the German Lutheran Church, Nile St.

Any such study is dependent on the help of librarians,
archivists and museum officials and we would like to
thank the following: Jill Crowther, Margaret Burwell,
Sara Donaldson and all the staff at Hull Local Studies
Library; Geoff Oxley, Susan Jones and staff at Hull City
Record Office; Keith Holt, Carol Boddington and staff
at Humberside County Archive Office; the staff of the
Borthwick Institute of Historical Research, University
of York; and Carolyn Aldridge and Susan Jeffrey of Hull
City Museums. Graham Edwards of the Hull City
Museums Design Department receives our thanks for
promptly and expertly copying the many illustrations
gathered in.

We are most grateful to Humberside County Archive
Service, Kingston upon Hull City Record Office, Hum-
berside Libraries (Hull Local Studies Library), the Hull
Daily Mail, Christopher Ketchell Collection, Sam Allon
Collection, Miss A. Dalheim, David Dixon, German
Lutheran Church Council, John Markham, Margaret
Palfreman, Robert Wise, Barbara Green, Geoff Bell,
Bernard Blanchard and Edward Ingram for permission
to use illustrative material. Others who kindly provided
information and/or illustrations include Jack Allerston,
Kenneth Beaulah, Miss Brown, Mgr. J.R. Charlton,
Mrs. Dixey, Fred Fletcher, Audrey Goodrum, Help!
Conservation Action Group, Local History Unit, Hull
College of Further Education, Josie Montgomery, Mrs.
Norah O'Brien, Leslie Powell, and Mike Tracey.

FOREWORD

Hull is proud of some recent developments to the city centre and skyline but there is much to regret. A new dome has arisen opposite the Guildhall and the old church of St. Mary Lowgate has been more clearly revealed. In the semi-circle of the inner city, around the civic and commercial centre, changes are not all so pleasing. Great attempts are being made to provide decent housing. New uses are being found for old schools; low-budget community centres are designed to serve mixed populations. Unfortunately handsome public buildings that resulted from a more stable tradition have proved too expensive to maintain. The corners of so many long streets of two storey dwellings, with their infill of face-to-face houses, were marked by spires, towers and cupolas. Behind these symbols of congregational prosperity and missionary zeal, halls and schools provided for the social needs of their adherents. Many of these churches and chapels were lost in the bombardments of two wars. More recently shifts of population, and the growth of vehicular traffic, have caused survivors to be changed to commercial or industrial usage. Some have been completely lost beneath flyovers or dual carriage-ways. In a number of cases grandiose temples have been replaced by car parks attached to succeeding buildings designed for cheaper upkeep.

We were anxious to record some of these changes before evidence was lost and memories fade. As a museum service, we aim to collect and preserve relics of social and religious life and we receive many requests to identify views and sites. Changing architectural taste may have contributed to the disregard for decorative variety so we thought it useful to record the battle of architectural styles and the imaginative mixtures of motifs adopted by the various sects. We were therefore very pleased to enlist the enthusiastic help of a group of knowledgeable historians.

Dr. David Neave, of Hull University, has provided most of the information about Nonconformist places of worship and written the comprehensive introduction. With the help of Dr. Susan Neave, he has compiled the lists of buildings and architects. Mr. A. G. Bell has supplied the details of the Anglican Churches and Mr. Chris Ketchell has supplied further information and illustrations from his store of local knowledge.

Many other local people have contributed souvenirs and memories and clergy and laity have helped with material which has passed to existing parishes and congregations. We are grateful to all who have helped our efforts to make the publication comprehensive and the exhibition visually stimulating.

The editorial team has not aimed at a religious history of Hull. Dr. Neave's introduction points at how difficult this is to unravel but enables us to understand the main sectarian developments. Whichever bank of the River Hull may be considered to be the more Christian side of the city, there can be no doubt of the importance of religious belief in the lives of so many citizens. We have attempted, in the exhibition, to try and convey something of the warmth that existed in both worship and social activities. The publication concentrates on the architectural record, the richness of decorative detail and furnishings now lost, the architects and the benefactors whose vision created such a varied skyline above our flat landscape.

The illustrations show a remarkable pattern of change and we realise this must continue, only wishing the future could bring as rich a heritage as the past. No-one wants today to see further continuation of sectarian rivalry and the churches themselves have discouraged expenditure on unnecessary embellishment. It would be wrong to divert public funds from more pressing social requirements and greater architectural tragedies. Nevertheless the exhibition may help everyone to pause and consider. We hope that the record will help planners, developers, clergy and congregations faced with the maintenance of public worship, to combine to find means to ensure the list of lost churches and chapels does not duly increase; that means will be found to prevent wholesale losses and the desecration of surviving architectural features. In essence we believe that this survey of the past will contribute to the future well-being of a rapidly changing community.

Trevor P. Larsen
Chairman, Cultural Services Committee.

John Bradshaw
Curator, Hull City Museums and Art Galleries.

October, 1991.

Although the majority of the losses recorded in the following pages took place in the twentieth century, churches and chapels have been disappearing from the landscape of Hull for over 400 years. Some thirteen churches or chapels existed in the area of modern Hull in the middle ages. Of these only three, Holy Trinity, St. Mary's, Lowgate and St. James's, Sutton, survive with much of their medieval fabric intact. The church of St. Peter, Drypool, no longer exists and St. Giles's, Marfleet, and St. Mary's, Sculcoates, have been rebuilt, the latter on a new site.

Little is known of the medieval chapels at Myton, destroyed in 1204, Southcoates, first mentioned in 1236, and Trippet, recorded in 1454. Nor are the exact sites known of the churches of Hull's three medieval religious houses which were dissolved in 1539. The Carmelite Friary (Whitefriars) is first mentioned in 1289 when it was sited on the south side of the present Blackfriargate. The friary was soon moved to a site on the south side of Whitefriargate where a new church was consecrated in 1311. The Augustinian Friary (Blackfriars) was founded in 1317; its site on the north side of Blackfriargate, is now crossed by the western approach road to Myton Bridge.

The site of Hull's Carthusian Priory, founded in 1378, was probably to the west of the present Charterhouse. The priory church, which contained the tombs of the Michael and William de la Pole, respectively 1st Earl and 1st Duke of Suffolk, had its origins in the chapel of the Maison Dieu founded by William de la Pole in 1354. The fine Georgian chapel of the present Charterhouse may be considered its successor.

The Reformation reduced the churches of the walled area of Hull to two, Holy Trinity and St. Mary's, and it was not until the later 17th century with the rise of nonconformity that places of worship began again to be built there.

Organised nonconformity in Hull had its origins amongst the Puritan and independent minded merchant community in the early 17th century. By the mid-17th century Independents, Presbyterians and Quakers were holding religious meetings in the town. The early dissenters generally met in private houses but during 1650's the Independent congregation had use of the chancel of Holy Trinity while the Presbyterians met in the nave. With the Restoration of Charles II and the return of the established church the nonconformists were again confined to secret meetings in private houses. The Quakers were particularly restricted from meeting together. Some of those found attending meetings were imprisoned and others physically abused.

In 1672 both the Independents and the Presbyterians took advantage of the Declaration of Indulgence and registered meeting-houses. In that year the Presbyterians built a meeting-house in Blackfriargate. Unfortunately, no illustration survives of this building, which was Hull's first purpose-built nonconformist place of worship, nor do we know of its exact location. It probably

Church of Augustinian Friary,
Blackfriargate, 1789. (HCMAG).

had a short life as a meeting-house for the Declaration of Indulgence was withdrawn in 1673 and for the next 15 years the town's nonconformists were vigorously pursued for not attending their parish church and for keeping conventicles.

The passing in 1689 of the Toleration Act which allowed for the licensing of dissenting meeting-houses led directly to the building of a Presbyterian Chapel in Bowlalley Lane in 1691-2 and the first Independent chapel in Dagger Lane in 1698. The Quakers who may have been meeting in Lowgate at the house of William Garbutt, one of their early followers, since at least 1678 acquired the property as a meeting-house in 1709. A fourth dissenting meeting-house was registered by the Baptists in 1717. From 1736 the Baptists met in the tower of the former King's manor house in Manor Alley.

In 1743 it was reported that some 300 people regularly attended the main weekly service of the Presbyterians in Bowlalley Lane, 200 the Sunday service at the Independent chapel in Dagger Lane, 60 the once weekly meetings at the 'Anabaptist' chapel in Manor Alley and some 45 people the Quaker meeting.

Soon these early dissenting groups were to be joined by a body that was to transform Hull's religious life. In 1746 Elizabeth Blow, a follower of John Wesley, arrived in Hull from Grimsby and made the first converts to Metnōdism in the town. Wesley himself paid his first visit to Hull in 1752 when he preached to a large crowd at Myton Carr. Rioting followed and Wesley was pursued to the town by a mob.

Such antagonism proved no hindrance to the movement and membership of Hull's Methodist Society increased rapidly. Meetings were initially held in private houses until, in 1761, the Methodists took over the tower in Manor Alley in succession to the Baptists. Ten years later they pulled the tower down and built a fine new meeting-house in its place. On a visit in 1772 John Wesley described the new Manor Alley chapel as 'extremely well finished, and upon the whole one of the prettiest preaching houses in England'. Within a few years this chapel was too small to hold his local followers and in 1787 the much grander George Yard chapel was built. This Wesley found to be 'well built and elegantly finished - handsome, but not gaudy'.

In the later 18th century Hull appears to have been gripped with religious fervour. The older dissenting sects experienced great doctrinal changes and their history is somewhat confusing. In 1757 the Presbyterian congregation meeting at Bowlalley Lane became and remained Unitarian. The Independent congregation at Dagger Lane however became Presbyterian on the arrival of a new minister in 1767. This caused some of the congregation to secede and found a new Independent chapel in Blanket Row in 1769. This was in turn replaced by the new Fish Street chapel in 1782. Then in the following year the Old Dagger Lane chapel became Swedenborgian and remained so until 1840.

The Baptists as well were riven by disputes between Arminians and Calvinists among their congregation. In 1757 they had built a new chapel in a yard off Salthouse Lane and in 1765 the Calvinist Baptist minister left with some of the congregation and six years later opened a new Baptist chapel in Dagger Lane. Ten years later this chapel passed to the Countess of Huntingdon's Connexion.

To this religious melting pot can be added Roman Catholicism and Judaism. Post-Reformation Catholicism was virtually non-existent in Hull until the later 18th century. Around 1778 the town's first known Roman Catholic chapel was built in Posterngate. It had a short life for it was partially destroyed by a mob in 1780 during an outburst of local anti-Catholic feeling aroused by the Gordon riots. It was not until 1799 that a new Roman Catholic chapel, in North Street, off Prospect Street, was registered.

The gutted Catholic chapel in Posterngate was taken over soon after 1780 by the Old Hebrew Congregation who repaired it and established there Hull's first Jewish synagogue. The Jewish community, which was to play such an important part in the history of Hull, had its origins in one Michael Levy, a watchmaker, who was registered in the town in 1770. Immigration increased

Hull's Jewish population as well as adding other cosmopolitan aspects to its religious life. A German Lutheran congregation was established by 1801 and to this were added in the 19th century Danish and Finnish Lutheran missions largely addressed at visiting seamen.

The rapid growth of dissent as well as the population of the town did not go unnoticed by members of the Anglican church but it was some years before they provided new churches. A strong evangelical tradition developed in the later 18th century at Holy Trinity and St. Mary's, Lowgate, encouraged by the Wilberforce and Thornton families. A succession of active evangelical Anglican clergy came to the town beginning with Joseph Milner (1744-97), headmaster of the Grammar School and lecturer at Holy Trinity. It was Milner's disciple the Revd. Thomas Dykes (1761-1847) who in 1791 personally funded the building of St. John the Evangelist, the first Anglican church to be built in Hull since the Reformation. Although an act of Parliament was secured to provide a new church in Sculcoates in 1814 it was not until 1822 that the second new church, Christ Church, was consecrated.

Meanwhile the number of nonconformist chapels had multiplied to serve the expanding working and middle-class residential areas to the west and north and across the River Hull to the east. The Methodists led the way and in the first quarter of the 19th century a dozen Methodist chapels were opened including, in 1814, the splendid Waltham Street Wesleyan chapel which could seat 1,500. The Methodist fervour in chapel building was partly engendered by the splits that had occurred in the movement since the 1790's.

The secession of Alexander Kilham to form the Methodist New Connexion in 1797 was partly the result of a letter entitled the 'Signal Gun from Hull' written by two local Methodists, Thomas Thompson and Richard Terry, who wished to retain links with the Church of England. The Methodist New Connexion built their first chapel in Hull in North Street (later Charlotte Street) in 1799. Other breakaway Methodist groups who opened chapels in Hull before the mid-19th century were the Independent Methodists, the Wesleyan Association, the Wesleyan Reformers, and by far the most important, the Primitive Methodists.

It was in 1819 that William Clowes, one of the founders of Primitive Methodism, returned to mission Hull where he had worked in a pottery fifteen years before. He met with immediate success and the first Primitive Methodist chapel was built in Mill Street in 1819. Hull soon became a major centre for Primitive Methodist mission work throughout England. Six chapels were opened in the town by the time of Clowes' death in 1851. He died in Hull and was buried in the General Cemetery on Spring Bank. The newly built chapel in Jarratt Street, with seating for 1,400, was named in his memory.

Details of three religious censuses taken in 1834, 1851 and 1881 record graphically the expansion of religious provision in Hull in the mid-19th century.

Of particular note is the expansion of the various Methodist sects who increased their chapels fourfold and the staggering attendances at the Salvation Army services in 1881. This body, whose founder William Booth had been ordained as a Methodist New Connexion minister in Hull's Bethel Chapel in 1858, was newly arrived in the town and seemingly its services were attracting great crowds. None of its meeting places were purpose-built and the largest in Cambridge Street, which accommodated 4,200 on the night of Sunday, October 30, 1881, was a converted ice-house.

More than 20 of the 108 recorded places of worship in 1881 were not purpose-built. The short-lived sects such as the Primitive Christians, the Christian Pioneers, the Soldiers of the Cross and the Christian Army of necessity met in hired halls and private houses. Such independent religious groups meeting in adapted premises have always played an important part in the city's religious life. This booklet however is primarily concerned with purpose-built places of worship and in particular those with some architectural merit. Hull had some of the finest chapels in Britain exhibiting the whole range of nonconformist architecture.

Church and Chapel Provision in 19th century Hull

	Churches and Chapels			Seating			Total Attendances		
	1834	1851	1881	1834	1851	1881	1834	1851	1881
Church of England	8	18	25	9800	14020	19300	6400	12229	13272
Roman Catholic	1	1	3	600	648	1310	450	1650	2414
Independent/Cong.	6	6	9	5750	4966	7175	3100	3680	4909
Presbyterian	-	1	4	-	600	2600	-	206	1882
Baptist	3	4	3	1700	1140	1330	1000	926	819
Wes. Methodist	7	10	22	5530	8212	13911	4760	7406	12504
Prim. Methodist	1	5	14	1250	2838	12650	1000	4962	9553
Other Methodist	2	4	6	1750	2762	3856	1050	3790	2230
Salvation Army	-	-	4	-	-	6050	-	-	11394
Others	5	9	18	1800	3545	5578	1090	3534	9161
Total	33	58	108	28180	38731	73760	18850	38383	68138

The earliest nonconformist chapels were plain rectangular boxes often tucked away in yards and it was not until the building of Manor Alley and George Yard by the Methodists that any architectural detailing appeared. The standard design of Manor Alley with its gabled facade and symmetrically placed round-headed openings was echoed in many Hull chapels well into the 19th century including Mill Street Primitive chapel of 1819. George Yard was more unusual with its seven bay, two storey facade and fine porticoed front door. In 1796 a similar elegant Georgian facade was provided at George Street Baptist chapel which had a central Venetian window and a matching doorway below.

In 1813-14 Hull Wesleyans built their largest chapel in Waltham Street. This splendid building which could hold 2,000 worshippers was designed by the first specialist Wesleyan chapel architect, William Jenkins of London, who was responsible for many fine chapels throughout England. Waltham Street, which was one of his most successful, had a flat Classical facade with round-headed windows and a large pediment. There were side pavilions and a large projecting portico. This basic design was copied locally in 1833 for Humber Street Wesleyan chapel and Salem Congregational chapel, Cogan Street each of which had a central pediment, round-headed windows and a prominent portico. That at Humber Street was Ionic while Salem's was in the Greek Doric style.

The Greek Revival style was most successfully utilised for Hull's two greatest chapels, Albion Street Congregational and Great Thornton Street Wesleyan, both designed by H.F. Lockwood in 1841-2. They are rightly considered to have been amongst the finest nonconformist chapels in the country. Other impressive Classical facades were provided at Kingston Wesleyan, 1841, Great Thornton Street Primitive, 1849, and Clowes Memorial Primitive, 1851.

It was in mid-century that the battle of the styles began in Hull nonconformist circles and the Gothic style was used for the first time. A rather debased Gothic had already been employed for the Betheseda Chapel in Osborne Street in 1842 echoing the Mariners Church of

1834. B.W. Blanchard has linked the introduction of a more correct Gothic style to the publication in 1850 of *Chapel and School Architecture* by F.J. Jobson, an architect and prominent Wesleyan minister. Jobson strongly advocated Gothic as the only true Christian architectural style. In 1857 the Hull architect William Botterill produced a version of one of the designs from Jobson's book for the modest Gothic Wesleyan chapel at Newland. Then in 1861 Botterill used the same source for his design for the much larger and more elaborate Beverley Road Wesleyan. The older dissenting groups were prepared to go further in their adoption of the Gothic and this can be seen with St. Andrew's Presbyterian church on Prospect Street of 1866, which was planned as a Free Church of England Church, and W.H. Kitching's Wycliffe Congregational Church on Anlaby Road of 1867. The latter had full traceried windows, nave, transepts, and a residual chancel. A tower and spire were added later. In 1871 the Primitive Methodists even succumbed to the Gothic, a style they traditionally linked with Catholicism, when they built the Bourne chapel on Anlaby Road. This building had little more than Gothic embellishments and the architect Joseph Wright and the Primitive Methodist Church to which he belonged were far happier using a free Italianate or Renaissance style. Striking examples of this style were to be found on Spring Bank with the Jubilee and Ebenezer Primitive chapels, on Beverley Road the Wesleyan chapel on Queens Road corner and along Holderness Road at Bright Street Primitive and Brunswick Wesleyan chapels.

Later in the century a free Gothic style predominated particularly at the hands of W. Alfred Gelder, Hull's most prolific chapel architect, and this culminated in such chapels as the Princes Avenue and Portobello Methodist chapels of 1905-6.

Gothic, as one would expect, was the style employed for the Anglican and later Roman Catholic churches although the first Anglican church to be built since the Reformation, St. John the Evangelist, Queen Victoria Square, had a typical austere Georgian exterior. It had little of the Georgian charm of the tiny St. Giles Marfleet rebuilt in 1793. The first Gothic churches, Christ Church, 1822, St. James, 1831, and St. John, Newland, 1833, showed little understanding of the style. More impressive were H.F. Lockwood's designs for the two churches of St. Mark's, 1844, and St. Stephen's, 1845, each dominated by a soaring spire, but even these show that the architect was much more conversant with the Classical style. By the late 1860's Hull architects such as Samuel Musgrave, R.G. Smith and F.S. Brodrick and the local born Edward Simpson of Bradford were producing far more competent works influenced by such national figures as William Butterfield, and G.E. Street, Street himself was responsible for All Saints, Margaret Street in 1869, chosen in preference to R.G. Smith of Hull who was considered by the Archbishop of York to be too inexperienced. At the end of the century another leading architect, George Gilbert Scott, the younger, who had strong Hull connections, designed St. Augustines. His design was in fact amended by his former pupil the equally accomplished Temple Moore. Fuller notes are provided on the architects of Hull's lost churches and chapels in Appendix B.

It would be impossible here to summarise adequately the history of church and chapel building in Hull. Well over a 150 purpose-built places of worship were opened in Hull between the years 1750 and 1920. Hundreds of thousands of pounds were spent on their building and maintenance and huge debts were incurred but paying these off gave a purpose to many congregations. In 1920 it was said that only 13 out of 38 Primitive Methodist chapels built in the previous hundred years had been completely paid for. Such debts existed despite the generosity of many Hull industrialists. The Hodge family donated thousands of pounds towards building Primitive Methodist chapels, and Joseph Rank and Thomas Ferens were equally liberal with regard to the Wesleyan cause. Major fund-raising events in the form of three-day bazaars, such as when Kingston Wesleyan chapel, Witham, was transformed into 'Venice in Hull' in March 1898, added greatly to the town's social life in the late

19th and early 20th centuries. The greatest social contribution of the city's lost churches and chapels was through their extensive educational provision for both children and adults. In the case of many of the chapels the area of their schoolrooms and institutes exceeded that of the place of worship.

Hull has lost much, both socially and visually, with the disappearance of so much of its religious heritage. Of the 115 purpose built places of worship existing in Hull in 1901 only 25 survive today of which 11 remain in use. A further 11 churches and chapels built in Hull between 1901 and 1920 also remain. (see Appendix A)

Methodist Union in 1932 led to the closing of many surplus chapels because the Wesleyans and Primitives had often built in close proximity to each other and vied to produce the grander building. The Second World War caused the greatest loss. At least 35 of the churches and chapels listed in the following pages were destroyed by bombing or so badly damaged that they were subsequently destroyed. The relocation of residential areas in the post-war years made many chapels redundant and others were cleared for housing or road improvements.

But not all have gone. Churches and chapels, or their associated buildings, have found new uses as masonic halls, a frozen food store, a wine store, a health centre, a nightclub, and various shops, workshops, and warehouses. Demolished churches and chapels have been replaced by housing, car parks or new roads as well as by shops, factories, petrol stations, car showrooms, a vehicle rental firm, and on rare occasions by new churches.

Some of the few remaining pre-1920 churches and chapels are today under threat. If they do close it is to be hoped that a sympathetic new use will be found that will retain their original appearance and ensure that they long continue to contribute to Hull's townscape bearing witness to a vital element of the past and present history of the city.

What is meant by a lost church and chapel? All the buildings included in the following gazetteer have been lost as places of worship and the majority have been lost from the landscape of the city. Included in the gazetteer are all known purpose built churches or chapels that were erected in Hull before 1920 which have either been demolished or are no longer used as a place of worship. Chapels associated with cemeteries or public institutions have not been included. In some cases the previous building on the site of a present place of worship has been included because of its architectural significance. Short-lived temporary structures which were later superseded have not been listed.

Abbreviations for captions:

Greenwood - J. Greenwood, *Picture of Hull*, Hull 1835.
HCAO - Humberside County Archive Office.
HCMAG - Hull City Museums and Art Galleries.
HLSL - Hull Local Studies Library, Humberside Libraries.
KHRO - Kingston upon Hull Record Office.
NHG - *New Hull Guide*, 1880.

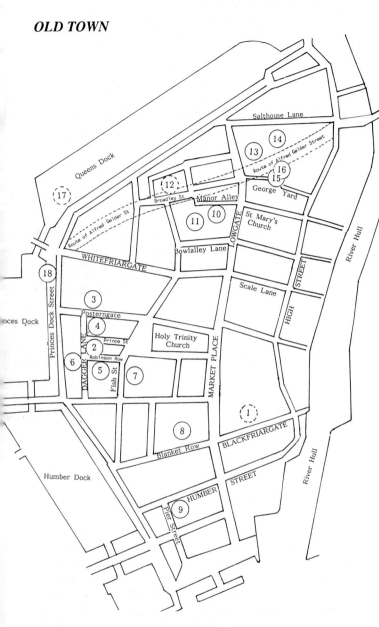

Sites of lost churches and chapels in the Old Town of Hull.
Street layout of c.1900. Numbers refer to sections of text on following pages.

1. BLACKFRIARGATE. Presbyterian. Hull's first recorded dissenting meeting-house was built in Blackfriargate in 1672. Only used for some 10 years. Site unknown.

2. DAGGER LANE. Old Dagger Lane Chapel. Built by Independents in 1698. Became Swedenborgian in 1783 when it was altered. Became Presbyterian in 1841. Replaced by Spring Bank in 1875. Used as a synagogue for a time. Acquired by Minerva Lodge of Freemasons who had been using adjoining schoolroom in Prince Street since 1809. Now part of Masonic Hall. Outside walls rebuilt 1978.

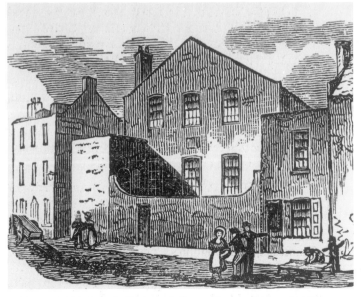

Old Dagger Lane Chapel (2), 1835. (Greenwood)

Roman Catholic Chapel, Posterngate (3), 1780.
(Diocese of Middlesbrough).

3. POSTERNGATE. Roman Catholic chapel built shortly before 1780. It was destroyed in the Gordon riots in 1780. Rebuilt as a Synagogue by the Jews shortly after. Closed 1826. Building used as a workshop in 1865. Victoria Chambers built on site in 1880's.

4. POSTERNGATE. Mariners' Church of the Good Shepherd. Built for the Hull Mariners' Church and Seamen's Rest Society 1926-27. Architect Thomas Snowden. Now used as Hull Post Office Club.

5. ROBINSON ROW. Jewish Synagogue built 1826. It was a small building down a narrow passage. Rebuilt fronting the street in 1852 to the designs of W.D. Keyworth. Replaced by Osborne Street in 1903. Used as a warehouse before demolition in 1928. Site in the centre of Trinity Court housing development.

6. DAGGER LANE. Ebenezer Chapel/Mariners' Church. Opened April 1771 by Baptists in secession from Salthouse Lane. Entry from Dagger Lane. Extended 20 feet west in 1776. In 1781 it passed to the Countess of Huntingdon's Connexion. Bought by Rev. Samuel Lane in 1804, described as Calvinist in 1823. Ebenezer renamed New Dagger Lane Chapel in 1826. Independent. Used as the Anglican Mariners' church 1828-34. Demolished and replaced by new church.

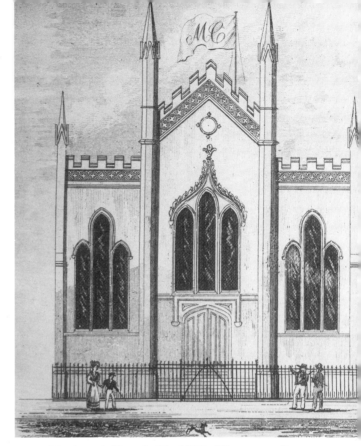

Mariners' Church (6), 1835. (Greenwood).

The MARINERS' CHURCH was established by William Hey Dykes (1794-1864) son of Revd. Thomas Dikes of St. John the Evangelists. In 1821 he founded the *Port of Hull Society for the Religious Instruction of Seamen.* Then in 1828 he established the Mariners' Church Society and purchased the former Ebenezer Chapel which was demolished in 1834. The new Mariners' Chapel opened on the site 15 June 1834. It was in the Gothick style, described by Greenwood as 'an indifferent specimen of Early English'. In use until c.1906. Later used as warehouse. Much altered building finally demolished November 1978. Site covered by the housing of Lisle Court.

Fish Street Chapel (7), 1869.

Fish Street Chapel (7), interior.

7. FISH STREET. Congregational chapel built in 1782, at cost of £1575, to replace Blanket Row. Enlarged in 1802 to contain 1,050 sittings. Restored and modernised, internally and externally in 1869. Replaced by Prince's Avenue in 1898. Chapel sold and later became a telephone exchange and then a warehouse. Demolished 1984. Site covered by housing to east of Fish Street.

8. BLANKET ROW. A short lived Independent congregation in secession from Old Dagger Lane built a small meeting-house in Barker's Court off Blanket Row. The building was enlarged 1773 before being burnt shortly afterwards and sold in 1783. It was the basket manufactory of John W. Beeton in 1864. Since demolished.

Wesley Chapel, Humber Street (9), 1835.
(Greenwood).

9. HUMBER STREET. Wesley Chapel. Built by Wesleyan Methodists in 1832-3. Designed by William Sissons of Hull and built at a cost of £3,600. It could seat 1300. Remodelled in 1887 and became Wesley Hall. Closed 1905 and it became a fruit auction room. Destroyed during Second World War. A fruit warehouse, nos. 66-8 Humber Street, is now on the site.

Manor Alley Chapel (10), c.1900. (HCMAG).

13. LOWGATE. The Society of Friends (Quakers) were probably meeting in William Garbutt's house in Lowgate from 1678. They acquired the house for meetings in 1709. A larger meeting-house was built in the yard behind in 1780. It had 390 sittings in 1851. Replaced by Mason Street in 1852. Building became Oddfellows Hall. Later demolished. Site opposite Guildhall.

14. SALTHOUSE LANE. Baptist chapel built in 1757 in yard to south of Salthouse Lane. Enlarged 1790, galleries were built round three sides and a recess for singers behind the pulpit. It had 550 sittings. Replaced by South Street in 1866 and was later demolished. Sunday school added c.1840. Site now housing on north side of Alfred Gelder Street.

10. MANOR ALLEY. A Baptist congregation founded in 1736 met in the tower of the former de la Pole Manor house until 1757. Taken over by Methodists in 1757 who demolished tower and built Manor Alley chapel on site in 1771. Replaced by George Yard in 1791. Used as a bonding warehouse in 1864 and demolished in early 20th century.

11. BOWLALLEY LANE. Presbyterian, then Unitarian. Replaced Blackfriargate c.1680. Rebuilt 1691/92 and again in 1802. The last building was a distinctive octagon with 490 sittings. Red brick octagon with windows in each side. Galleried nearly all round. Replaced by Park Street Unitarian in 1881. Became offices before being demolished in 1936. Site to the north of Cogan Chambers in Exchange Alley.

12. BROADLEY STREET. Congregational mission room established c.1865. It had seating for 230 in 1881. Registered until 1896. Demolished.

Bowlalley Lane Chapel (11), 1887.
Drawing by F.S. Smith (HCMAG).

GEORGE-YARD CHAPEL, *founded A.D. 1786.*
under the Patronage of The Rev.d John Wesley. — *To whom*
This PLATE is humbly dedicated *by his obed.t humble Serv.t* Tho.s Briggs

George Yard Chapel (15). (G. Hadley, History of Hull, 1788.).

15. GEORGE YARD. George Yard Methodist chapel. Built c.1785 at a cost of £4,500. 1,060 sittings in 1851. Red brick with stone dressings. A seven-bay two-storey building with round-headed windows throughout with Gothic style glazing bars. The centre three bays projected nine inches and had a porticoed central door with segmental pediment. Secondary doors gave access to galleries and side aisles. The galleries which were supported by fluted oak columns ran round three sides. The high mahogany pulpit which was opposite the entrances was flanked by high windows. The ceiling had attractive plaster detailing. The chapel was modernised in 1891. Closed November 1905 and demolished soon after.

George Yard Chapel (15) interior after 1891.
(HCMAG).

George Yard Chapel (15) interior with pulpit before 1891. (HCMAG).

16. ALFRED GELDER STREET. Queen's Hall, Wesleyan. Replaced George Yard Chapel in 1905. Designed by Sir Alfred Gelder in a Free Gothic style it could seat 2,000. It cost £20,000. Opened September 1905, closed 1960 and demolished June 1965.

17. QUEEN'S DOCK. The 'Valiant' Floating chapel. An interdenominational chapel founded in 1821 by the Port of Hull Society in the hulk of the Valiant. The vessel had formerly been a Dutch ship 'Cornelius and Maria' captured in 1803. It could seat 500. The vessel was usually moored at the west end of Queen's Dock but was later moved to Prince's Dock. Dispensed with in 1849 and later broken up.

18. NEW DOCK STREET. Baptist/Unitarian chapel shown on west side of New Dock Street on Anderson's map in 1818 as 'Sleepers Chapel'. Presumably demolished when Prince's Dock was built in 1829.

Queen's Hall, Alfred Gelder Street (16). (C. Ketchell).

Floating Chapel (17), 1835 (Greenwood).

CENTRAL HULL

Area bounded by Freetown Way to the north and Ferensway to the west.

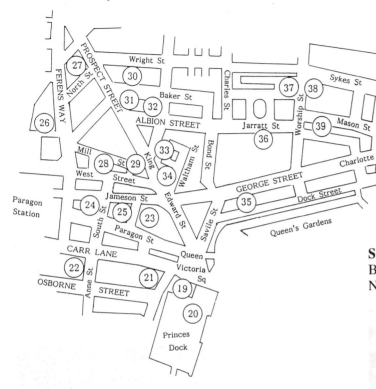

Sites of lost churches and chapels in Central Hull.
Based on a street plan of c.1950.
Numbers refer to sections of text on following pages.

St. John the Evangelist Church (19), c.1875. (HCMAG).

St. John the Evangelist Church (19), c.1840. (HCMAG).

19. QUEEN VICTORIA SQUARE. St. John the Evangelist Anglican church. This church, consecrated in 1792 and opened in 1793, was built as a chapel-of-ease to Holy Trinity to serve the expanding population to the west of the Old Town in the district called Myton. The church, the first post-Reformation Anglican church to appear in Hull, was built by the evangelical clergyman Revd. Thomas Dykes (he spelt his name Dikes) using his own fortune. It was partly financed by pew rents and payments for the use of over 70 burial vaults under the church. A chancel and west tower were added in 1803. The chancel was remodelled by Cuthbert Brodrick in 1863 and in 1874 a plan was produced by Christopher Wray, architect of the Dock Offices opposite, to convert the church into a High Renaissance building. The latter was not carried out. It had seating for 1,670 in 1881 and was the largest Anglican church in Hull. The church was assigned its own district in 1868 and closed in 1917, when it was bought by T.R. Ferens and presented to Hull Corporation so that an art gallery might be built on the site. The building was demolished when the site was cleared to build the Ferens Art Gallery, construction of which began in 1924.

Proposed alterations to interior of St. John's (19) by Christopher Wray, 1874. (HCMAG).

St. John's Church (19) looking west from behind pulpit, c.1900. (HCMAG).

St. John's Church (19) gallery, c.1900. (HCMAG).

17

20. PARADE ROW. Jewish synagogue in use from c.1820. Sold 1826 and demolished for building Princes' Dock opened 1829.

21. OSBORNE STREET. Built by a Baptist congregation in 1823 but taken over by the Independent Methodists in 1826. Restored c.1865 when given an Italianate stuccoed facade. It was taken over by Methodist New Connexion in 1876. Sold to Freemasons in 1904. Damaged in war and later demolished. Allders store is now on the site.

22. OSBORNE STREET (Anne Street). Jewish synagogue opened in 1903 replacing Robinson Row. Enlarged 1932. Badly damaged by bombing in 1941 and rebuilt 1955. Entrance in Anne Street. Closed and now part of the Studio Circus Nightclub.

23. HOPE STREET. Providence Independent chapel. (Congregational). Built 1797 restored in mid 19th century. Seating for 1,150. The building was almost hidden from view between the end of Hope Street, a court off Chariot Street, and Chapel Street. The last taking its name from this building which was almost square in plan with galleries. The pulpit, which was situated between the main doors to Hope Street, was replaced by a large platform in 1860. Closing service was held October 1903. The building was subsequently used as a warehouse. Destroyed by bombing in 1941. No known illustration of exterior exists. Site now part of the Queens House site (between Chapel St. and King Edward St.).

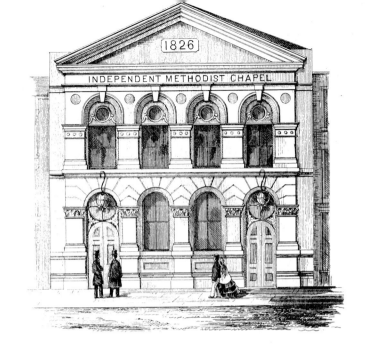

Independent Methodist Chapel, Osborne Street (21), c.1865. (HCMAG).

Jewish Synagogue, Anne Street (22), 1989. (Hull Daily Mail).

24. SOUTH STREET. Baptist chapel built privately in 1840. Used by various denominations including Baptists, Primitive, Methodist New Connexion and Wesleyan Reformers, until 1866 when Baptists from Salthouse Lane moved there. Seating for 800. Closed 1903. Since demolished. TSB bank on site.

25. PARAGON STREET. Christian Temperance church on corner of Paragon Street and Little Queen Street. Foundation stone laid 17 April 1843. Used by Baptists and then by Latter Day Saints in 1851. Became warehouse. Demolished c.1935. Site now offices.

26. MOXON STREET. Hamilton Place. Independent (Congregational) chapel opened 1839 in Hamilton Place, a court off Moxon Street. Seated 200. Became Hope Street Congregational schoolroom. Taken over as chapel by Free Methodists in 1860. Closed by 1876. Subsequently used by Wesleyans. Demolished in 1930. Site north of Ferensway Bus Station.

27. NORTH STREET off Prospect Street. Roman Catholic chapel built 1799. Closed 1829 when replaced by St. Charles Borromeo. Demolished before 1866. Site now at rear of Shirethorn Centre on Prospect Street.

Baptist Chapel, South Street (24), 1887.
Drawing by F.S. Smith (HCMAG).

Roman Catholic Chapel, North Street (27).
(Diocese of Middlesbrough).

Christian Temperance Church, Paragon Street (25).
(HCMAG).

Mill Street (West St.) Primitive Methodist Chapel (29)

28. MILL STREET. St. Patrick's Roman Catholic chapel. School-chapel built in 1871. Seating for 350. Closed in 1906. School remained. Demolished. Site part of car park.

29. MILL STREET. West Street Primitive Methodist chapel. Built 1819 at cost of £1,700. Seating for 790. First Primitive building in Hull. Set back in a yard. Simple two storey three bay building with pedimented gable. Galleried interior. Closed 1910. Building then used as a dance hall. Destroyed by bombing in 1941. Chapel site in the yard north of Woolworths.

30. BAKER STREET. Free Church of England church opened in 1844 on north side of Baker Street. Became church hall in 1866 on the building of a new church on Prospect Street (later St. Andrew's Presbyterian church) Hall rebuilt 1890. Now carpet and furniture warehouse.

31. PROSPECT STREET. St. Andrew's Presbyterian church. Built for Free Church of England congregation in 1866. Acquired by Presbyterians in 1868. Built of stone in Decorated style. Architect A.D. Gough of London. Seating for 850. Badly damaged in air raid in 1941. Central Library built on site.

Mill Street (West Street) Primitive Methodist Chapel (29) interior, 1902. (HLSL).

*St. Andrew's Presbyterian Church, Prospect Street
(31), 1898. (HLSL).*

*St. Andrew's Presbyterian Church, (31)
interior, 1898. (HLSL).*

Independent Chapel, Albion Street (32), 1842. (HLSL).

32. ALBION STREET. Albion Independent chapel (Congregational). Foundation stone laid 7 July 1841. Opened 1842. Cost £8,000. Designed by H.F. Lockwood in Greek Revival style. The front elevation consisted of a massive stone Doric portico of six columns. Stone front, side and rear walls of grey brick with stone surrounds to the windows. Internally the galleries were supported on square iron pillars with Grecian capitals. Seating for 1642. Organ installed in 1849. Below the chapel were schoolrooms and burial vaults. Largely destroyed by bombing in 1941. Remaining part demolished 1949. Insurance office built on site at corner of Percy Street.

Albion Chapel (32) after bombing, 1941. (KHRO).

33. SCHOOL STREET. Jewish synagogue opened in 1887. Replaced by Cogan Street in 1914. Demolished.

34. WALTHAM STREET. Wesleyan chapel opened October 1814. Designed by William Jenkins in Classical style. Cost £9,000. Seating originally for 1,500. Built of brick. Stuccoed facade. Interior had apse for organ (fitted 1832) behind pulpit. Gallery on all sides. Round-headed windows throughout and circular windows on either side of pulpit. New entrance from King Edward Street in 1902. Closed for regular worship in 1932. Damaged in Second World War and demolished in 1949. Methodist Central Hall built on site in 1960.

35. GEORGE STREET. Baptist chapel built 1796 at cost of £1,200. Seated 600. Altered 1842 when brickwork at front was stuccoed. Interior altered in 1854 and 1860. Last service held November 1903. Building became Prince's Hall Cinema in 1910. Later a club which was demolished 1985. At present (Oct. 1991) a redevelopment site at 38 George Street.

*Wesleyan Chapel, Waltham Street (34), 1835.
(Greenwood).*

*Baptist Chapel, George Street (35), 1835.
(Greenwood).*

*Wesleyan Chapel, Waltham Street (34),
interior, 1898. (HLSL).*

36. JARRATT STREET (Kingston Square). Clowes Primitive Methodist chapel built 1851. Designed by William Sissons in Greek revival style, built of red and grey brick with stone dressings. Pilastered facade with large triangular pediment. Internally the side pews faced one another across auditorium. Fine Greek style mouldings including the plaster ceiling roses. Seating for 1,400. It cost £7,410. Closed 1932 and used as a warehouse. Demolished February 1965. Site now occupied by the former Hull Brewery building known as Kingston Gardens.

37. WORSHIP STREET. Christ Church. This Anglican church, consecrated in 1822, the first chapel-of-ease in the parish of Sculcoates, was built so that those living in the southern part of the parish could attend worship without having to travel to the parish church of St. Mary, Sculcoates in Air Street, an unpleasant journey particularly in winter. The church was designed by William Hutchinson of Hull. White stock brick with dressings of Roche Abbey stone. In Perpendicular style. A chancel and vestry to the south by William Kerby were added in 1863. The church had seating for 1600. The church was assigned its own district in 1886. Though badly damaged by bombing in 1941, services continued under the south gallery until 1952. The building was demolished in 1962. The site is now the car park behind the New Theatre. Christ Church Schools, designed by Cuthbert Brodrick in 1849, survive next to the car park.

Clowes Primitive Methodist Chapel (36), Jarratt Street. (HCMAG).

Christ Church, Worship Street (37), 1855. (HCMAG).

Christ Church (37) showing extension and chancel by William Kerby, 1863. (NHG).

38. SYKES STREET. Tabernacle. Independent chapel opened 1827. Used by a succession of denominations from 1835: Wesleyans, Presbyterians, Wesleyan Association, Methodist Free Church, Congregational, Reform Methodists, New Connexion Methodists, and Primitives. Seating for 1000 in 1881. Closed c.1900. Destroyed in Second World War. Site under Freetown Way.

Tabernacle, Sykes Street (38), 1883, on left with Christ Church in distance.
Drawing by F.S. Smith. (HCMAG).

39. MASON STREET. Wesleyan chapel built 1826. Simple three bay two storey facade with pediment and two single storey wings with arched window openings. Entrance portico. Acquired by Quakers in 1851 and after enlargement was opened as a meeting house in 1852. It was galleried on three sides and could seat 600. Became schoolroom in 1880 when adult school and new smaller meeting house were built on site adjoining to east. Closed 1918. Became a warehouse. Demolished in 1970's. Site now part of car park.

40. MASON STREET. Jehovah Jireh Baptist chapel built in 1822 on Little Mason Street. Small, square building with hipped roof. Said to have been sold to the Wesleyan Association in 1837 and to have been used by Primitive Methodists. Was a Wesleyan Association chapel in 1856. In 1859 it became the Trippett Anglican school. Front was stuccoed. Schools closed in 1909 and subsequently demolished. Its site adjoins the Charterhouse burial ground.

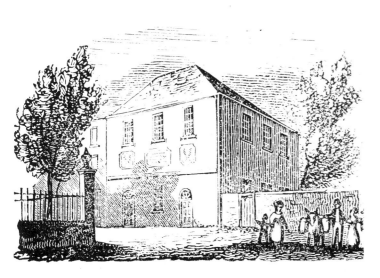

Jehovah Jireh Baptist Chapel,
Little Mason Street (40), 1835. (Greenwood).

St. Philip's Church, Charlotte Street, (41), 1883. (HCMAG).

41. CHARLOTTE STREET. St. Philip's Anglican church. The church was consecrated in 1885 to serve a district assigned in that year from the parish of Sculcoates, the extra-parochial territory of the Charterhouse and Trippett, then in Holy Trinity parish. The architects were Botterill, Son and Bilson. Red brick with stone dressings in Early English style. The church was badly damaged by bombing in the Second World War, its vicar, Canon Sedgwick, being killed in his church. The building was then demolished. The site, where Carroll Place (formerly Paradise Row) meets George Street (formerly Charlotte Street), is at present derelict.

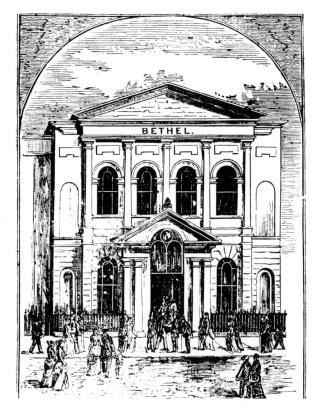

Bethel Methodist New Connexion Chapel, Charlotte Street (42), after 1875. (HCMAG).

42. NORTH STREET. (later Charlotte Street). Bethel Methodist New Connexion chapel. Built 1799. A small square chapel with porticoed entrances. Front altered in 1875 when given Italianate detail. Seating for 800. The chapel was destroyed by bombing in 1941. Its site is at the junction of Freetown Way, George Street and Wilberforce Drive.

Sites of lost churches and chapels in West Hull.
Based on a street plan of c.1950.
Numbers refer to sections of text on following pages.

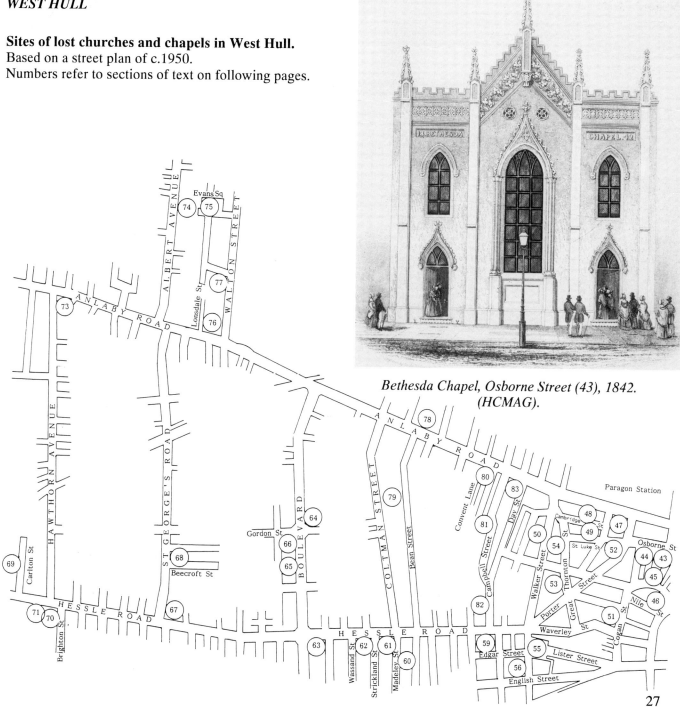

Bethesda Chapel, Osborne Street (43), 1842.
(HCMAG).

27

43. OSBORNE STREET. Bethesda chapel. Built 1842 as an Independent chapel in a crude Decorated style similar to the Mariners' Church. Seating for 500. Taken over by Danish Lutherans in 1850.

Rebuilt as St. Nicolai's Danish Lutheran church in 1871. Designed by William Botterill. Destroyed by bombing in 1941. Hanover Court later built on site. New church built on other side of street.

St. Nicolai Danish Lutheran Church (43).
(HCMAG).

44. LOWER UNION STREET. Wesleyan chapel built 1820. 280 seats. Closed in 1840s. In use by Independent Methodists in 1851. Used by Wesleyans again in later 19th century. Became a Jewish mission hall and a synagogue from 1928 until damaged by bombing in 1941. Still in use by Jewish youth organisations in 1964. Since demolished. Hanover Court flats now on site.

45. LOWER UNION STREET. Wesleyan mission room opened 1882. Designed by Botterill, Sons and Bilson. In use until 1910 then an Independent Methodist chapel 1911-c.1930. From 1933 it was St. Victor's undenominational chapel. Closed February 1968. Demolished. Housing now on site.

Wesleyan Mission Room, Lower Union Street.
(45), 1898. (HLSL).

German Lutheran Church, Nile Street (46) in mid 1890s. Church built 1827; 1848 was the year in which Hull German Lutheran Church was founded. (Copyright A. Dalheim, Hull).

German Lutheran Church, Nile Street (46) 1913. (Copyright German Lutheran Church Council, Hull).

46. NILE STREET. Trinity Independent chapel. Built 1827 and used by the Independents until 1842. It was then used by Baptists 1845-7, and Primitive Methodists 1847-9, before becoming St. Luke's Anglican Church for a period in 1856. Then in 1858 it was acquired by the German Lutherans.

German Lutheran services were being held in Hull by 1801. The present Hull German Lutheran Church was founded in the winter of 1847-8. Services were first held in the Sailors' Institute, Waterhouse Lane, and later in the Bethesda Congregrational Chapel, Osborne Street. The first service was held in the newly acquired Nile Street Church in April 1859. The church was described in J.J. Sheahan's *History of Hull* (1864) as 'a small neat structure of red brick. The interior is neatly pewed, and has galleries on three sides. Against the east wall is the pulpit and beneath it within an enclosed space, is a plain table covered with dark velvet. This is called the altar, and on it stands a handsome crucifix in a neatly mounted base, and two candlesticks containing candles'. A bell tower was added in 1882.

By 1910 the building was too small to accommodate an expanding congregation. It was demolished and a new church, designed by Oswald Hillerns, was constructed at a cost of £1,577 in a simplified Gothic style. The first service was held on the 22 March 1911. On the outbreak of the Great War services ceased and the building passed into the care of the Osborne Mission. It reopened on a restricted basis on 22 June 1933, but it was not until 4 July 1935 that the Lutherans regained full possession of the building. During the Second World War the church again closed, being used by Clover Dairies until mid 1948. Services recommenced on 19 June 1949.

The church was compulsorily purchased and demolished in the mid 1960s to make way for the construction of the South Orbital Road. The site now lies under the Mytongate roundabout.

St. Luke's Church, 1886 (49).
Drawing by F.S. Smith. (HCMAG).

Salem Congregational Chapel, Cogan Street (51),
1835. (Greenwood).

47.   ANLABY ROAD. Ice House Citadel, Salvation Army. Established 1897, replaced Cambridge Street. Closed 1989 and at present disused.

48.   CAMBRIDGE STREET. Former Ice house taken over by Salvation Army in 1881. Seating for 3,500. on Sunday October 30, 1881, 4200 attended the evening service. Used until 1892. Then sold for conversion into a people's palace and art gallery.

49.   ST. LUKE STREET. St. Luke's Anglican church. The church was built as a chapel-of-ease to Holy Trinity and consecrated in 1862, gaining its own district in 1864. The church replaced a temporary church, first in a disused chapel in Nile Street and then in Porter Street. The architect was Robert Blessley of London. Red brick with black bands and stone dressings in Early Decorated style. A tower by R.G. Smith and F.S. Brodrick was added in 1878. The church was badly damaged in the Second World War and demolished. The site is now occupied by council housing.

50.   WALKER STREET. Zion chapel. Built by Wesleyan Reformers c.1855. Replaced by Campbell Street in 1866. Registered by Independent Methodists 1871-76. Taken over as Zion Calvinist chapel by 1881 and in use until 1930. 250 sittings.

51.   COGAN STREET. Salem Congregational chapel. Built 1833 in Classical style at a cost of £3,000. Probably designed by William Sissons. Seating for 950. Burial vaults below. Sold to Jews for a Synagogue in 1914, replaced by West Parade in 1940 and destroyed during Second World War.

52.   PORTER STREET. Chapel built by the Independents in 1851. Taken over by Wesleyan Reformers in 1853. Used as St. Lukes Church by Anglicans 1856-62. Then the building was sold and after substantial rebuilding was opened as the Alhambra Music Hall in 1864. Renamed the Hippodrome in 1905 and became a cinema in 1913. Destroyed by bombing in 1941. The site is now a triangular area of grass opposite Turner Court.

53. GREAT THORNTON STREET. Wesleyan chapel. Built 1842 at a cost of over £7,000. A magnificent Greek Revival building designed by H.F. Lockwood of Hull. Could seat 1,400 (1881). Stone facade with brick sides and back. One of Hull's finest buildings it was largely destroyed by fire in 1907. One wing survived into the 1950s. Replaced by THORNTON HALL.

THORNTON HALL. Wesleyan Mission opened in 1909 on site of Great Thornton Street Chapel. Designed by Gelder and Kitchen. Cost £18,250 and could seat 2,000. Badly damaged by bombing in 1941 and subsequently demolished.

Wesleyan Chapel, Great Thornton Street (53), c.1900. (David Dixon).

Thornton Hall (57) after blitz, 1941. Note surviving pavilion from earlier chapel to left. (KHRO).

A SNAPSHOT IN CONFERENCE: THE DEBATE ON THE TWENTIETH CENTURY SCHEME.

Interior of Wesleyan Chapel, Great Thornton Street (53) during Wesleyan conference, 1898. (HLSL).

*Primitive Methodist Chapel, Great Thornton Street
(54), second chapel after damage by bombing in
1941. (KHRO).*

54. GREAT THORNTON STREET. Primitive Methodist chapel built in 1849 to rival nearby Wesleyan Chapel. Designed by William Sissons in Italianate style. Cost £5,178. Burnt down in 1856 and subsequently rebuilt with altered facade. Seating for 900. Closed 1937 and damaged by bombing in 1941 and subsequently demolished.

*Primitive Methodist Chapel, Great Thornton Street
(54), first chapel of 1849. (HCMAG).*

55. ST. JAMES SQUARE, LISTER STREET. St. James's Anglican church. This church, consecrated in 1831, was built as a chapel-of-ease to Holy Trinity to serve the expanding population in the area of Hull, south of Hessle Road, known as the Potteries. The church was only assigned its own district in 1874. Designed by J.A. Hansom (of Hansom cab fame) and E. Welch, the church was a Commissioners' Church its building being financed partly by government money and partly by Hull Corporation. White Wallingfen stock bricks with stone dressings in Early English style. It had seating for 1000. Major alterations were made to the interior in 1866, 1871 and finally in 1931 when the galleries were removed. The church was closed in the mid 1950s and demolished in 1957. The site is now a garden.

St. James's Church (55), c.1900. (HCMAG).

56. ENGLISH STREET. Wesleyan chapel built 1818 on corner of St. James Street. Closed 1831 and later demolished. Industrial building on site.

57. ALFRED STREET. Wesleyan chapel built 1831 to replace English Street. Closed 1851. Exact site unknown.

58. ST. MARK'S SQUARE. Wesleyan chapel opened in Potteries in 1806. Replaced by English Street by 1818. Exact site unknown. A later chapel-like building is incorporated in Shears McGrath fishcurers premises.

59. EDGAR STREET. Built by Primitive Methodists in 1891 at cost of £400 adapting existing premises first mentioned in 1872. Seated 220. No longer in use in 1954. Demolished. Stood on corner of Mechanics Lane.

60. MADELEY STREET. Salvation Army Citadel. Built 1888. Demolished 1983. Site alongside Clive Sullivan Way flyover.

Primitive Methodist Chapel, Hessle Road (61), 1991.

61. HESSLE ROAD. Primitive Methodist chapel built in 1881 at cost of £8,200. Most costly Primitive chapel in Hull. Designed by William Freeman in Romanesque style. Seating for 1,000. Closed 1933 and building taken over by Elim Church in 1934 who renamed it the City Temple. Closed 1984 when City Temple moved to Prince's Avenue. Chapel empty and increasingly derelict.

St. James' Church (55), interior. (HLSL).

Congregational Chapel, Hessle Road (62), 1875. (HCMAG).

62. HESSLE ROAD. Congregational chapel built 1875-7 at cost of £6,500. Red brick Gothic building designed by Samuel Musgrave. Seating for 900. Closed 1949. Used by an amateur theatre group until 1954. Demolished by 1964. Petrol station on site.

63. HESSLE ROAD. St. Barnabas Anglican church. The church was consecrated in 1874 and assigned its own district from Holy Trinity in that year. The site was given by Henry Strickland Constable and the buildng was designed by Samuel Musgrave. Red stock brick with stone dressings in Early English style. The church was closed in 1970 and subsequently demolished. The site near the Fishermen's Memorial, on the corner of South Boulevard is now occupied by housing.

St. Barnabas Church, Hessle Road (63), 1881. (HCMAG).

St. Barnabas Church, Hessle Road (63), interior. (Hull Daily Mail).

64. BOULEVARD. United Methodist church opened September 1907 designed by W.H. Bingley. Red brick with yellow brick details. Some similarities to Fish Street Memorial Congregational Church, Prince's Avenue, by same architect. Closed in 1960s and demolished since 1985. Nursing home on site.

65. BOULEVARD. St. Wilfrid's Roman Catholic church built 1896 at cost of £3,000. Designed in Gothic style by Smith, Brodrick and Lowther. Destroyed by landmine in March 1941. Replaced by new church in 1956.

66. GORDON STREET. Boulevard Baptist church. Built in 1903, at cost of £12,000, to replace South Street. Designed by T.B. Thompson in Gothic style, of yellow brick with red-brick dressings. Demolished early 1970's. Prefabricated church built on site. Adjoining Sunday School and Institute of 1904 survive on Gordon Street.

Boulevard Baptist Church, Gordon Street (66), c.1970. (R. Wise).

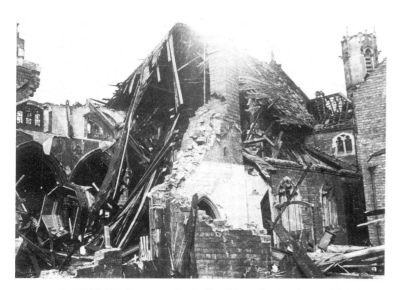

St. Wilfrid's Roman Catholic Church, Boulevard (65) after destruction by land mine, 1941. (KHRO).

United Methodist Church, Boulevard (64), 1907. (HCAO).

St. George's Road Wesleyan Chapel, Hessle Road (67), 1898. (HLSL).

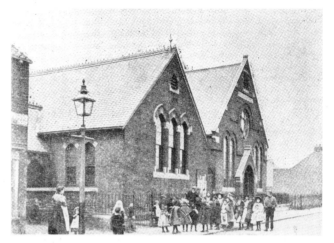

Wesleyan Mission Room, Carlton Street, (69), 1898. (HLSL).

67. HESSLE ROAD. St. George's Road Wesleyan chapel. Built in 1883 at cost of £4,000, replacing a building registered in 1877. Designed in Italianate style by T. Brownlow Thompson. Red brick. Chapel enlarged and schoolrooms built at back in 1904 to designs of Gelder and Kitchen. Became the Thornton Hall (St. George's) Mission in 1942. Closed. Demolished June 1981. Kwik Save Supermarket on site.

68. ST. GEORGES ROAD. (Beecroft Street). Small Primitive Methodist chapel built 1873 designed by William Freeman in Gothic style. Cost £850, seating for 200. New larger chapel also by William Freeman built alongside in 1889-90. Cost £3,646, seating for 650. Earlier chapel became schoolroom. A further large schoolroom was added in 1898 to designs of T. Brownlow Thompson. Chapel closed 1966 and since demolished. Site remains as open space.

69. CARLTON STREET. Wesleyan mission room built 1865 at cost of £500. Designed by William Botterill in simple Gothic style. Seating for 300. Replaced by larger chapel in 1886. Closed 1962 and demolished 1968/9. Site now warehouses. (Green's Components).

Primitive Methodist Chapel, Beecroft Street, St. George's Road (68), 1902. (HLSL).

Waltham Street Wesleyan Chapel, Hull watercolour by S. Norman, 1816. (HCMAG).

Great Thornton Street Wesleyan Chapel, Hull. (HLSL).

70. BRIGHTON STREET. Primitive Methodist mission hall built in 1889. 440 sittings. Cost £557. Demolished. New road over site.

71. HESSLE ROAD. St. Mary and St. Peter's Anglican church, Dairycoates. The church was consecrated in 1902 to serve a district taken from Newington parish, and eventually assigned in 1906. It was designed by W.S. Walker of the Hull firm of Brodrick, Lowther and Walker. Red brick with terracotta mouldings in Romanesque style. The church was deconsecrated in 1962, a replacement church on the opposite side of Hessle Road being consecrated on the same day. This new church added to an existing hall and designed by Hull architect Allanson Hick was closed 1969 and has subsequently been demolished. The old church building was taken down in February 1962 to make way for the Hessle Road flyover which replaced the Dairycoates level crossing.

72. HESSLE HIGH ROAD. St. Nicholas's Anglican church. This church was consecrated in 1915 to serve a district assigned in that year from the parish of Hessle. The church, designed by Hull architect John Bilson, was given by Christopher Pickering as a memorial to King Edward VII. Red brick with stone dressings in Perpendicular style. Sadly the demolition of this church was ordered in late 1967, the foundations having become unsound. It has been replaced by the present church of St. Nicholas. Not shown on plant - Ordnance Survey ref. TA 053270.

73. HAWTHORN AVENUE. Norman Memorial Primitive Methodist church built 1905 to designs of T. Beecroft Atkinson at cost of £4,900. In multi-coloured brick. Destroyed by bombing 1941. Housing now on site.

St. Mary & St. Peter's Church, Hessle Road, (71).
(Hull Daily Mail).

St. Nicholas's Church, Hessle High Road (72),
1915. (HCAO).

Church of Transfiguration, Albert Avenue (74)
(The Church in King's Town, 1924).

Newington Presbyterian Church, Anlaby Road
(76), c.1900. (HCMAG).

74. ALBERT AVENUE. Church of Transfiguration. This Anglican church was consecrated in 1904 to serve a district eventually assigned from the parish of Newington in 1906, however the west front was not completed until 1915. The architect was F.S. Brodrick. Red brick with stone dressings in Decorated style. This permanent church replaced a temporary building originally used as a mission hut for the navvys who built the Hull and Barnsley Railway. In the early 1970s the church was closed, the congregation moving to share Anlaby Road Methodist Church on the corner of Plane Street. The church was demolished in 1975. The site is now occupied by housing.

75. EVANS SQUARE. (Lees Walk, Beetonville). Wesleyan mission hall in Gothic style built 1867. Grey brick with red brick and stone details. Major alterations in 1885. 300 sittings. Closed 1954 and demolished c.1960. Site covered by modern housing Lees Walk, Lowther Street off Walton Street.

76. ANLABY ROAD. Newington Presbyterian church. Built 1893 on south east corner of Lonsdale Street to replace Walton Street mission hall. Italianate facade designed by W.A. Gelder. Sold 1961 and demolished 1964. Site now shops with offices above. Schoolroom designed by T.B. Thompson c.1911 survives behind as Lonsdale Community Centre.

77. WALTON STREET. Presbyterian mission hall in use by 1881. Replaced by Anlaby Road chapel in 1893. Continued to be used as a place of worship. Enlarged in 1961 by the Christian Brothers. Demolished for housing in January 1984 and replaced by a new building.

Portobello Primitive Methodist Chapel,
Holderness Road, Hull. Elevation by
Gelder and Kitchen 1905. (KHRO).

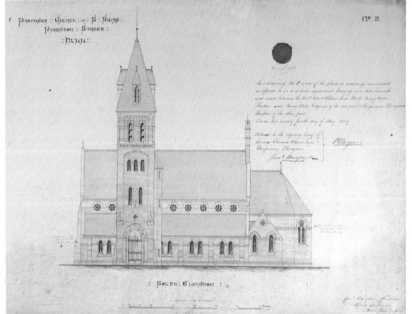

St. Silas' Church, Barmston Street.
South elevation by Samuel Musgrave
1869. (HCAO).

Bourne Primitive Methodist Chapel, Anlaby Road (78), 1869. (HCMAG).

78. ANLABY ROAD. Bourne Primitive Methodist chapel. Foundation stone laid September 1869. Designed by Joseph Wright of Hull. In white brick with stone dressings in Gothic style. Cost £7,610. Said to seat 2000 in 1881. Deregistered in 1960 and demolished by 1964. Miles Kingsport showroom on site (Oct. 1991). Schoolroom survives behind. 'Internally it is a most comfortable place of worship'. (Bulmer 1892). Named after Hugh Bourne, one of the founders of the Primitive Methodist Connexion.

79. COLTMAN STREET. Trinity Wesleyan chapel. Opened May 1872. Built at a cost of £8,000 to designs of William Botterill of Hull. Decorated Gothic style in Ancaster stone it could seat 1,250. Sunday school built at rear c.1895, designed by Gelder and Kitchen. Chapel damaged by bombing in 1941 and demolished in 1953. Coltman St. Day Hospital on site, opposite Wesley Court.

80. ANLABY ROAD. Roman Catholic Convent of Sisters of Mercy. Founded 1856 and rebuilt 1874 to designs of G.A. Goldie of London. Closed 1931 and destroyed by bombing in 1941. Remains demolished 1954.

Wesleyan Chapel, Coltman Street (79), 1898. (HLSL).

Convent of Sisters of Mercy, Anlaby Road (80) after bombing in 1941. (KHRO).

St. Thomas's Church, Campbell Street (81), 1873. (HCMAG).

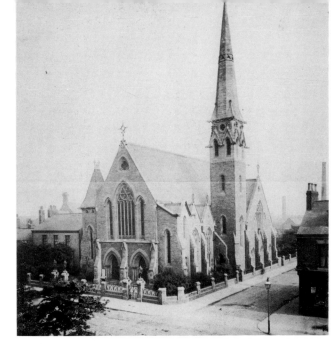

Wycliffe Congregational Chapel, Anlaby Road (83), c.1885. (HLSL).

Wycliffe Congregational Chapel (83) interior, c.1885. (HLSL).

81. CAMPBELL STREET. St. Thomas's Anglican church. A temporary church was opened in 1873, the permanent church being consecrated in 1882, when the church gained its own district from Holy Trinity. The building was designed by Edward Simpson of Bradford. Red stock brick with stone dressings in Early English style. The church was damaged in a Zeppelin raid in the First World War and more severely by bombing in the Second World War. The church was subsequently demolished. The site is now lost under council housing.

82. CAMPBELL STREET. Methodist Free Church built in 1866 at cost of £2,566. Designed by W. H. Kitching in Gothic style. Of grey 'Wallingfen bricks' with red brick string course. Seating for 556. Closed 1943 and since demolished. Housing on site.

83. ANLABY ROAD. Wycliffe Congregational chapel. Opened 1868. Built at a cost of £9,000 to designs of W. H. Kitching. Tower and spire by same architect added 1875. 1,100 sittings. Gothic style. Closed in 1935 and demolished January 1939.

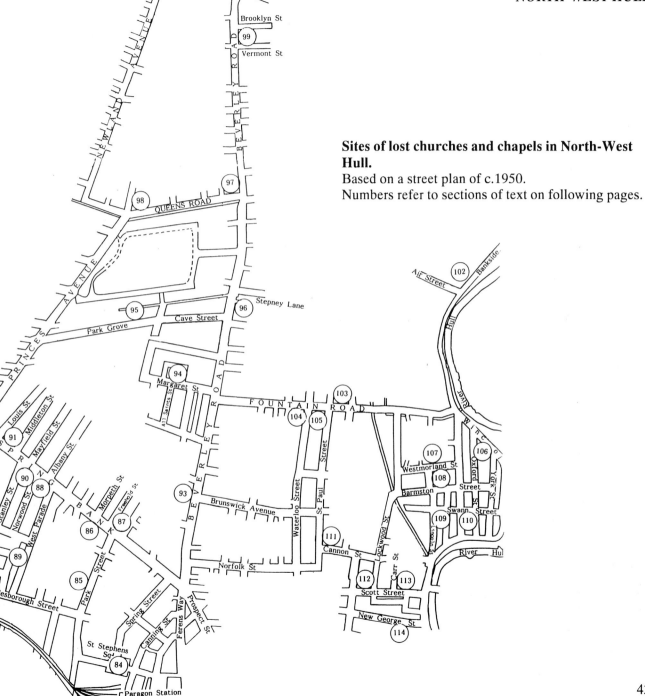

Sites of lost churches and chapels in North-West Hull.
Based on a street plan of c.1950.
Numbers refer to sections of text on following pages.

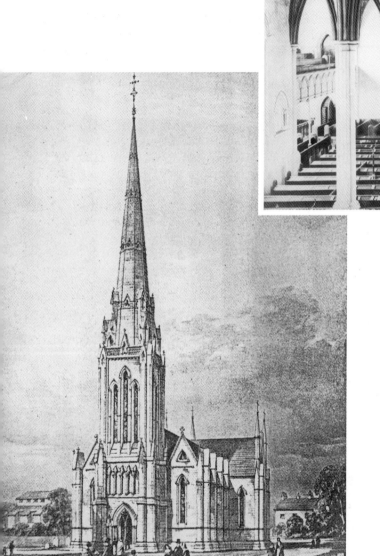

St. Stephen's Church (84) interior. (HLSL).

84. ST. STEPHEN'S SQUARE. St. Stephen's Anglican church. The church, consecrated in 1845, was built as a chapel-of-ease to serve that part of the parish of Holy Trinity known as North Myton. The church was eventually assigned its own district in 1859. Designed by Hull architect H.F. Lockwood, the building was the most elaborate Victorian church in Hull. Built of stone in Early English style. The church with its spire, a well known landmark behind Paragon station, was damaged during the Second World War, but its shell and spire survived until demolition in 1955-6. The site is now a garden. After the church was bombed, services continued in St. Stephen's Parish Rooms, now part of the Spring Street Theatre.

St. Stephen's Church (84). (HLSL).

Unitarian Church, Park Street (85). (M. Palfreman).

85. PARK STREET. Unitarian church built 1881-82 at cost of £4,000. Designed by W.H. Kitching in Gothic style. Of white brick with stone dressings. It had a spire at the north-east corner. Demolished c.1976 and replaced by a new church on the site in 1977.

86. SPRING BANK. Presbyterian church built 1875 at cost of £3,300. Designed by Smith and Brodrick of red brick in Gothic style. Seating for 500. Closed 1931 and demolished 1966. Site at present Kwik Fit tyres.

87. SPRING BANK. Jubilee Primitive Methodist chapel. Foundation stone laid February 1863, opened April 1864. Designed by Joseph Wright in the Italianate style. Of red and white brick with stone dressings. Cost £6,100 and had seating for 1,030. Renovated 1952. Demolished 1958 and replaced by new building in 1959 designed by B.W. Blanchard. This became the present St. Stephen's Anglican Church consecrated December 1972. Former Methodist schoolroom survives as church hall.

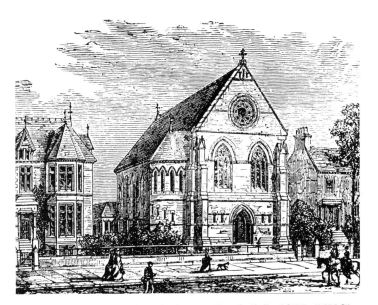

Presbyterian Church, Spring Bank (86), 1875. (NHG).

*Jubilee Primitive Chapel, Spring Bank (87).
(B.W. Blanchard).*

88. SPRING BANK. New Jerusalem church (Sweden-borgian) built 1875. Architect unknown. Red brick with stone dressings in Gothic style. Seating for 280. First minister was the distinguished local antiquarian J.R. Boyle. The church closed in 1948 and is now a second-hand furniture warehouse (Hull Clearance Centre).

89. WEST PARADE. (off Spring Bank). Wesleyan mission room opened 1874. Seating for 400. Closed 1895 but continued to be used as a Sunday school for Argyle Street Wesleyan until 1910. It was the Dreadnaught cinema 1912-22. Still standing as a ware-house in 1964. Demolished in 1970s. Housing on site.

90. SPRING BANK. St. Jude's Anglican church. The church was consecrated in 1874 and assigned its own district from Holy Trinity in that year. The building was designed by Edward Simpson of Bradford. Red brick in Early English style. Seating for 800. The parish was united with that of St. Stephen in 1957 with St. Jude's as the parish church. In 1973 this united parish was merged with the parish of St. Augustine, the rebuilt Jubilee Methodist Church being bought by the Church of England to become the parish church of St. Stephen the Martyr, Sculcoates. The Church of St. Jude was then closed and demolished. The site is now a car park for the frozen food store part of which occupies a building which was St. Jude's parish hall designed by C.D. Allderidge of Hull in 1925.

Former Swedenborgian Church, Spring Bank (88), 1991.

St. Jude's Church, Spring Bank (90)
(The Church in King's Town, 1924).

Ebenezer Primitive Methodist Chapel, Spring Bank (91). (C. Ketchell).

91. SPRING BANK. Ebenezer Primitive Methodist chapel built 1877-8 at a cost of £8,060 to designs of William Freeman. Of white brick with stone dressing with what a contemporary report called a 'Greco-Italian front capped with pyramids'. The distinctive Italianate facade incorporated French Renaissance detailing. Seating for 1000. Closed by August 1944. Demolished 1976. Site now yard for vehicle hire firm (Dennis Taylor).

92. ARGYLE STREET. Wesleyan chapel built 1895 at cost of £5,500. Designed by W.A. Gelder in Romanesque style with seating for 1000. Red brick with terracotta details. Clsoed 1959 and demolished by 1964. Site now a walled yard adjoining the former schoolroom added in 1910 to designs of Gelder and Kitchen which survives.

Ebenezer chapel (91). Harvest Festival, 1905. (C. Ketchell).

Wesleyan Chapel, Argyle Street (92), 1898. (HLSL).

Wesleyan Chapel, Beverley Road (93), 1860.
(HCMAG).

All Saints' Church, Margaret Street (94).
(HCMAG).

93. BEVERLEY ROAD. Wesleyan chapel. Opened January 1862. Built at a cost of £5,900 to the designs of William Botterill. An elaborate Gothic pinnacled facade with richly traceried five-light window. The gable was topped with a small octagonal turret and spire. It was built of white Wallingfen bricks with Brodsworth stone dressings. Seating for 1060. Closed in 1941 and used as a printing works before being destroyed by fire in 1954. The front wall with piers and gates survive. The school and class rooms built in 1865 at rear of the site are now used as a masonic hall.

94. MARGARET STREET. All Saints' Anglican church. Consecrated in 1869, this church immediately became the parish church of Sculcoates. The church was built to a design by G.E. Street after the Archbishop of York had rejected a design by Hull architect R.G. Smith because it exhibited his 'general inexperience'. Red stock brick with stone dressings in Early English style. The tower, by Hull architect Samuel Musgrave was added in 1883. Seating for 1100. The church was replaced as parish church of Sculcoates by the Church of St. Stephen the Martyr, Spring Bank, formerly the rebuilt Jubilee Methodist chapel, in 1972. The old church was closed, and demolished in 1974. The site is now occupied by housing (Cavendish Square).

95. PARK GROVE. French Convent of the Canonesses Regular of St. Augustine. Built 1914-15 to designs of Frederick A. Walters, architect of Buckfast Abbey. Demolished 1975. Now housing.

96. BEVERLEY ROAD. Stepney Methodist New Connexion chapel. Built in 1869 at cost of £2,500. Designed by William Hill of Leeds in the Gothic style. Had a corner tower and spire with a highly ornamented three light window in facade. Of red and white brick with stone dressings. Seating for 600. Sunday school block added in 1878. Closed 1966 and demolished before 1982. Kwik Save supermarket is on the site. Stepney chapel was built to replace Zion Methodist New Connexion chapel of 1849 which still survives on the corner of Cave Street.

Stepney Methodist New Connexion Chapel, Beverley Road (96). (NHG).

97. BEVERLEY ROAD. Queen's Road Wesleyan chapel. Built 1878 at cost of £9,000. Designed by Samuel Musgrave in Italianate style. Seating for 1200. Schoolrooms added in 1896. Damaged in air raid in Second World War. Chapel became a warehouse and services held in adjoining schoolroom. Closed 1967. Buildings demolished. Site now Queen's House flats.

Queen's Road Wesleyan Chapel, Beverley Road (97), (NHG).

*St. Augustine's Church, Queen's Road (98),
c.1960. (A.G. Bell).*

*St. Augustine's Church, Queen's Road (98),
view of proposed building by G.G. Scott, 1887.
(HCAO).*

98. QUEEN'S ROAD. St. Augustine of Hippo Anglican church. The church was consecrated in 1896 to serve a district assigned to it from Newland. A temporary church had existed on the site from 1884. The original plans were drawn up in 1887 by George Gilbert Scott, junior, but the work was eventually carried out by his assistant Temple Moore who produced a new design. Red brick relieved by tiles with stone dressings. In Decorated (Curvilinear) style. The proposed tower was never completed. The west porch was by H. Andrew. After closure the church was demolished in 1976. The site is now occupied by housing. Former church hall of 1901-2 by John Dossor survives.

99. BEVERLEY ROAD. Newland Congregational church. Foundation stone laid November 1904, opened 1906. Designed by Moulds and Porritt of Bury, Manchester and London in a Free Gothic style. Of red and yellow brick with terracotta dressings. The building was much criticised in Hull for its break from Nonconformist tradition. The church which was octagonal in plan with a huge dome-like roof was unusual in having a side pulpit and chancel. The corner tower and spire, 120 feet in height, had terracotta statues on the corner buttresses fifty feet up. The church was demolished 1969 except for the east end which has been adapted for services.

*Newland Congregational Church, Beverley Road
(99), (C. Ketchell).*

Newland Wesleyan Chapel (100), c.1900. (HCMAG).

Newland Wesleyan School Chapel, Newland Avenue (101), 1901.

100. COTTINGHAM ROAD. Newland Wesleyan chapel. Built 1857-8 on the corner of Newland Avenue at a cost of £600. Designed by William Botterill in Gothic style. Seating for 200. Closed in 1900 when school-chapel built opposite. Building used by Port of Hull Society until c.1962. Chapel demolished 1966. Site occupied by German Lutheran Church and pastor's house.

101. COTTINGHAM ROAD. Newland Wesleyan school-chapel, Newland Avenue. Built in 1901 to designs of Gelder and Kitchen at cost of £7,700. Seating for 850. New church built alongside in 1928. School-chapel largely demolished and car park now on the site.

102. AIR STREET. St. Mary's Anglican church, Sculcoates. This church, the ancient parish church of Sculcoates, is first mentioned in 1232. A drawing of c.1725 is said to show the medieval church which was replaced c.1759 by a new building which has been described as rococo Gothic in appearance but essentially Classical. Considerable alterations were made to this church in 1827-30, and again in 1861-3, in the latter case by William Botterill of Hull. In 1869 the church was replaced as parish church of Sculcoates by the newly built Church of All Saints, Margaret Street. The old church was again assigned its own district in 1873, before demolition c.1916 when it was replaced by the new Church of St. Mary in Sculcoates Lane. The new building incorporated much material from the old church, the tower of which long survived the demolition of the rest of the building. The churchyard remains though many gravestones have been removed.

St. Mary's Church, Sculcoates (102).
Drawing by F.S. Smith (E. Ingram).

*King's Hall Wesleyan Mission, Fountain Road (103).
(C. Ketchell).*

*Zion Primitive Methodist Chapel, Fountain Road
(104), 1902. (HLSL).*

103. FOUNTAIN ROAD. King's Hall Wesleyan mission. Built 1910 at cost of £18,000. Designed by Gelder and Kitchen. Seating for 2,000. Replaced a mission chapel adapted from former Liberal Club which had been first registered as a place of worship in 1895. King's Hall was closed in 1968 and demolished June 1970. Housing now on the site.

104. FOUNTAIN ROAD. Zion Primitive Methodist chapel. Built in 1877 at cost of £6,417. Designed by Joseph Wright in Italian Romanesque style. Seating for 800. Institute block added alongside 1909. It had extensive school rooms behind. Damaged by bombing in 1941, closed 1959 and demolished c.1960. Housing on site.

105. ST. PAUL'S STREET. St. Clement's Anglican church. A mission church of St. Clement in the parish of St. Paul, Sculcoates was opened in 1879, a new wooden mission room being opened in 1881. The church was used as a chapel-of-ease for many years but was never replaced by a permanent building although a church with an interior of Byzantine appearance was planned. After the church was closed the wooden building was demolished in 1937. The site is now lost under housing.

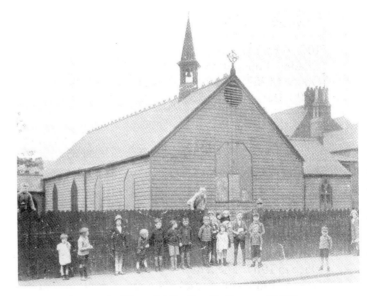

*St. Clement's Church, St. Paul's Street, (105).
(A.G. Bell).*

Former Primitive Methodist Chapel, Wincolmlee (106), 1991.

St. Silas' Church, Barmston Street (108), after damage by bombing, 1941. (KHRO).

106. WINCOLMLEE. Primitive Methodist chapel on former Church Street. Built 1842 replacing chapel opened initially by Primitives in 1819 in the 'Old Penitentiary'. Subsequently two houses nearby were used before the Wincolmlee chapel was built near York Street. Extended in 1846 to include Sunday school rooms. Closed in 1872 the building subsequently became a warehouse. Used as first Salvation Army barracks c.1879-80. At present (Oct. 1991) it is a warehouse owned by House of Townend. Facade unaltered.

107. WESTMORLAND STREET. Salvation Army Citadel. Foundation stones laid 10 December 1881. Opened 1882. Built of red brick in military style. Seated 2,500. Destroyed by bombing in 1941. Warehouse now on the site.

108. BARMSTON STREET. St. Silas's Anglican church. The church was consecrated in 1871 to serve a district assigned from the parish of St. Paul, Sculcoates in that year. In 1869 the Hull architect R.G. Smith won the competition for a design for the church but as in the case of All Saints', Margaret Street, he was replaced - this time by Samuel Musgrave. Red stock brick with stone dressings in Early English style. The last service took place in 1967. The redundant building was damaged by fire in 1968 and demolished the following year. A warehouse (engineering and welding supplies) is now on the site.

St. Silas' Church, (108), interior. (A.G. Bell).

Samuel Hodge Memorial Primitive Methodist Chapel, Lincoln Street (109), 1902. (HLSL).

109. LINCOLN STREET. Samuel Hodge Memorial Primitive Methodist chapel. Built 1872 at a cost of £5,300. Designed by Samuel Musgrave in Gothic style. Seated 950. Schoolrooms built 1902. Closed 1935 and subsequently demolished. Part remained in 1964. Workshop now on the site.

110. OXFORD STREET. Wesleyan mission hall built 1870. Seated 400. Closed 1910 and building used as the Oxford cinema and then offices. Demolished by 1964. Warehouse now on the site.

111. ST. PAUL STREET. St. Paul's Anglican church. The church, consecrated in 1847, was built to serve a district created from the parish of Sculcoates in 1844. The church was designed by William Hey Dykes, alterations being made to the furnishings in 1877 by Smith and Brodrick. Built of stone in Early English style. Seated 950. After several attempts to reduce the size of the building after the Second World War, including the demolition of the steeple in 1958, the church was eventually demolished in 1976 being replaced by a new building almost on the same site. This new church remains in use.

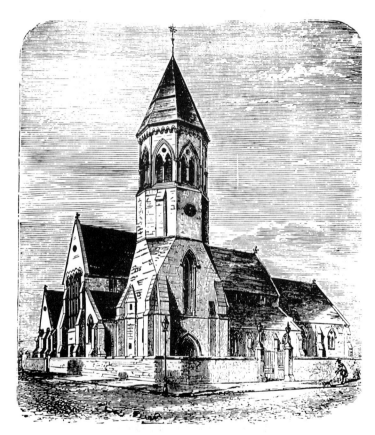

St. Paul's Church (111). (NHG).

St. Paul's Church (111) interior. (C. Ketchell).

Former St. Gregory's Roman Catholic School Chapel, Scott Street (112), 1991.

112. SCOTT STREET. St. Gregory's Roman Catholic school-chapel 1893 by R.G. Smith and F.S. Brodrick. Chapel on first floor with Gothic windows. Only used as a chapel for a few years. Now workshop on west side of Lockwood Street.

113. SCOTT STREET. Wesleyan chapel built 1804. Seating for 600. Rebuilt 1850 when front stuccoed. Further alterations by William Botterill in 1859. Closed 1910. Became printing works. Still standing in 1991.

114. NEW GEORGE STREET. Primitive Methodist mission room opened 1884 and used until 1922. Later demolished. Housing on site.

Former Wesleyan Chapel, Scott Street (113), 1991.

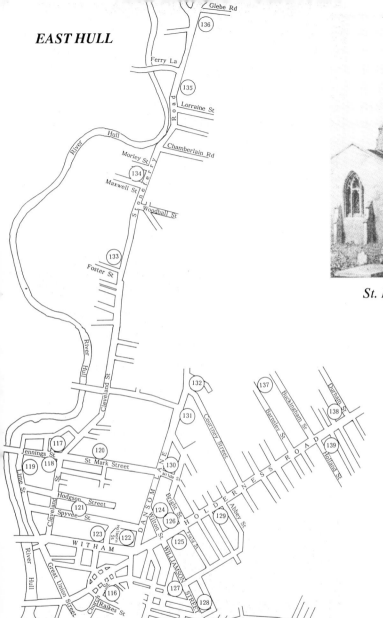

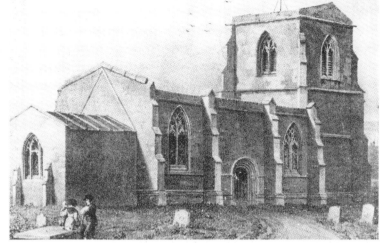

St. Peter's Church, Drypool (115), 1822. (HCMAG).

115. DRYPOOL. St. Peter's Anglican church. The first record of this church, the ancient parish church of Drypool, is in 1226 when the advowson was granted to Swine Priory. Pictures of the medieval church before its destruction c.1822 illustrate features that suggest the building may have existed by the 12th century. This medieval building was replaced, in 1823, by a new church designed by William Hutchinson of Hull. Built of brick rendered to imitate stone in Perpendicular style. The chancel was rebuilt in 1867 by D. Watson Aston. In 1878 the Church of St. Peter became a chapel-of-ease to the newly built Church of St. Andrew, Holderness Road which became the parish church of Drypool. The Church of St. Peter gained its own district again in 1879. The building was destroyed by bombs in 1941, but its shell survived the war, the tower being the last part to be demolished. The churchyard is now a garden.

Sites of lost churches and chapels in East Hull.
Based on a street plan of c.1950.
Numbers refer to sections of text on following pages.

*St. Peter's Church, Drypool (115),
after bombing in 1941.*

Wesleyan Chapel, Lime Street (119). (HLSL).

116. RAIKES STREET. Drypool. Wesleyan chapel. Built 1805 with seating for 250. Closed 1930 and was used as a workshop in 1964. Since demolished and site incorporated into a timber yard.

117. JENNING STREET. Wesleyan chapel on corner of Hood Street. Built 1818. Closed 1834 and later demolished. Site now club car park.

118. JENNING STREET. Groves Wesleyan chapel. School-chapel built 1896. Designed by Gelder and Kitchen in Gothic style, it incorporated fittings from Lime Street. Seating for 600. Damaged by bombing in 1941 and subsequently demolished. The site is now a factory yard.

119. LIME STREET. Wesleyan chapel. Built 1826 with seating for 340. Closed 1841 and subsequently used by various Methodist groups. It survived as a storehouse in 1964 but has since been demolished. Industrial buildings now on the site.

*Groves Wesleyan Chapel, Jenning Street (118),
after blitz, 1941. (KHRO).*

St. Mark's Church (120). (HCMAG).

120. ST. MARK STREET. St. Mark's Anglican church. The church was consecrated in 1844 to serve a district east of the River Hull assigned from Sutton together with the extra-parochial area of Garrison Side, an area known as the Groves. The building was designed by H.F. Lockwood of Hull, the transepts being altered in 1881 by the Hull architects R.G. Smith and F.S. Brodrick. Red brick with stone dressings in Early English style. It had seating for 1115. The top 25ft. of the spire was lost in a gale in December 1863. Later the spire was partially removed and, in 1938, the lantern was rebuilt. The church was badly damaged in the Second World War and closed in 1948. It was demolished in 1958-9 and its site is now used to store timber.

121. HODGSON STREET. Primitive Methodist chapel. Built in 1884 at cost of £1,450. Designed with minor Gothic detailing by W.A. Gelder. Seating for 260. Closed c.1940. Damaged by bombing. Incorporated in factory but chapel still identifiable in October 1991.

St. Mark's Church (120) interior. (C. Ketchell).

Primitive Methodist Chapel, Hodgson Street (121), 1902. (HLSL).

122. WITHAM. Kingston Wesleyan chapel. Built 1841 at cost of £8,000. Designed by James Simpson in Greek Revival style. Built in brick it had a stone facade with pediment supported on four massive Ionic pillars. The pulpit adjoined the front wall. Seating for 1,750 (1881). Damaged by bombing in 1941 and later demolished. Site now a petrol station and car showroom.

Kingston Wesleyan Chapel, Witham (122), 1898. (HLSL).

The Revd. J. Caughey preaching in Kingston Chapel, 1843. (KHRO).

Holborn Street Congregational Chapel, Witham (123), 1835. (Greenwood).

St. Mary's Roman Catholic Church, Wilton Street (124) interior. (C. Ketchell).

123. WITHAM. Holborn St. Congregational chapel. Built 1830 for the son of a minister of Hope Street chapel. Square hipped-roof building with two storey block at front with sloping roof. Burial vaults below the main building. Used by Primitive Methodists 1860-64. It then became a temperance hall before being used by the Salvation Army, Spiritualists and other religious groups. Converted to commercial premises and used as a grocery store in 1954 and an office equipment shop in 1991.

124. WILTON STREET. St. Mary's Roman Catholic church. A school-chapel was built in 1856 with seating for 360. The church was built alongside in 1890-91 to the designs of Smith, Brodrick and Lowther. In Gothic style. Demolished 1982. Warehouse now on site.

125. HOLDERNESS ROAD. Presbyterian church. Built 1874. Designed by W.H. Kitching in Gothic style. Of red brick with yellow-brick and stone dressings. Seating for 1100. Damaged by bombing in 1941 and services continued in adjoining Sunday school until 1949. Church demolished June 1972. Site now The Green Man public house which incorporates former schoolroom.

Presbyterian Church, Holderness Road (125). (NHG).

126. HOLDERNESS ROAD. Bright Street Primitive Methodist chapel. Opened 1864. Designed by Joseph Wright in Italianate style. Centre block had six Corinthian pilasters. Built of red and white brick with stone dressings at a cost of £5,116. Seating for 1,200 (1881). Damaged by bombing in 1941. Derelict in 1954 and demolished 1959-60. Site now a car showroom.

127. WILLIAMSON STREET. Latimer Congregational chapel. Built 1874 at cost of £2,500 replacing temporary building opened in 1869. Designed by Samuel Musgrave in Gothic style with patterned brickwork on facade. Corner tower and spire. Seating for 600. Taken over by Port of Hull Society in 1919. Later used as commercial premises. Demolished. Site now factory on corner of Strawberry Street.

128. WILLIAMSON STREET. Hodge Memorial Primitive Methodist chapel. Built 1873 at cost of £7,300. Seating for 1,400. Designed by F.N. Pettingell in Gothic style. Built in red brick with blue and yellow brick and stone dressings. Closed 1940 and used as a warehouse in 1964. Since demolished and site part of a haulage yard.

Bright Street Primitive Methodist Chapel, Holderness Road (126), 1902. (HLSL).

Latimer Congregational Chapel, Williamson Street (127), 1877. (HLSL).

Henry Hodge Memorial Primitive Methodist Chapel, Williamson Street (128), 1902. (HLSL).

129. HOLDERNESS ROAD. St. Andrew's Anglican church. Consecrated in 1878, this church became the parish church of Drypool in that year, replacing the Church of St. Peter. The church, designed by Adams and Kelly, ceased to be the parish church in 1961 when that title passed to the newly rebuilt Church of St. Columba further down Holderness Road. Built of red brick with stone dressings in Geometrical style. The church continued as a chapel-of-ease until closed prior to demolition in 1983-4. The site on the corner of Abbey Street is now occupied by housing.

130. WILDE STREET. Free Methodist chapel. Foundation stone laid by James Reckitt on 18 September 1876. Seating for 300. Closed 1911. Building survives incorporated into Reckitt and Colman's factory.

131. DANSOM LANE. Wesleyan chapel. Built 1876. Seating for 340. Closed in 1929 and remaining part is now Reckitt and Colman's Health Centre.

St. Andrew's Church, Holderness Road (129), 1960. (E. Ingram).

Former Free Methodist Chapel, Wilde Street (130), 1991.

St. Andrew's Church (129) interior, 1981. (A.G. Bell).

132. DANSOM LANE. Courtney Street Baptist church. Built as a mission hall in 1899. Red brick with pebble-dashed panels. It became a separate church in 1916. Closed. Still survives as workshop and warehouse.

133. STONEFERRY ROAD. St. Saviour's Anglican church. The church was consecrated in 1903 to serve a district assigned in 1904 from the parishes of Sutton and St. Mark. The permanent church designed by Brodrick, Lowther and Walker replaced an iron building dedicated in 1898, which survived as the church hall until both were demolished in 1981. Built in red brick with terracotta dressings in Early English style. The site, on the north side of Foster Street, has recently been used as a trailer park.

134. STONEFERRY ROAD. Emmanuel Primitive Methodist chapel. Built 1871 at cost of £822. Architect Joseph Wright. Closed 1962. Demolished since 1964. Site now industrial premises between Maxwell and Morley Streets.

135. STONEFERRY ROAD. Bethel Wesleyan chapel. Built soon after 1820, altered in 1836 and rebuilt in 1839. It had seating for 90. It was closed in 1892. Part of building was incorporated in Stoneferry Road School. Demolished.

Former Courtney Street Baptist Church, Dansom Lane (132), 1991.

St. Saviour's Church, Stoneferry Road (133). From the south-east, 1981. (A.G. Bell).

136. STONEFERRY ROAD. St. John's Wesleyan chapel. Built 1892 to designs of W.A. Gelder. Gothic detail. Seating for 100. Later enlarged. Demolished February 1986. Rievaulx Court built on site.

St. John's Wesleyan Chapel, Stoneferry Road (136), 1983. (C. Ketchell).

137. BARNSLEY STREET. Wesleyan mission hall. Built 1894-5 to the designs of W.A. Gelder. Seating for 340. Extended 1914, plans by Gelder and Kitchen. Destroyed by bombs in 1941. Housing on site.

138. HOLDERNESS ROAD. Brunswick Wesleyan chapel. Built 1877 at cost of £4,500. Designed by Samuel Musgrave in Italianate style. Front elevation had a pediment with Corinthian columns linked by semi-circular arches. Seating for 920. An assembly hall designed by W.A. Gelder was added in 1886 at cost of £3,000 and an educational institute by Gelder and Kitchen in 1903 at cost of £5,000. Chapel demolished in 1960 and replaced by new Holderness Road Methodist Church in 1962. Part of earlier complex survives to west and part of the schoolrooms at rear on Durham Stret.

139. HOLLAND STREET. Bethesda Primitive Methodist chapel. Built 1902 at a cost of £6,437. Designed by Gelder and Kitchen. Seating for 550. Closed 1962 and since demolished. Housing now on site.

140. PORTOBELLO STREET. Portobello Primitive Methodist chapel. Built 1906 at cost of £4,500. Designed by Gelder and Kitchen in Free Gothic style. Built of red 'Accrington' brick. Demolished 1984. Site now a car park for the new chapel which was converted from former hall.

Brunswick Wesleyan Chapel, Holderness Road (138), 1941. (KHRO).

Bethesda Primitive Methodist Chapel, Holland Street (139), 1902. (HLSL).

Portobello Primitive Methodist Chapel (140). (A.G. Bell).

141. HEDON ROAD. St. Bartholomew's Anglican church. This church, originally built as a sacristy for Drypool cemetery on Hedon Road, was licensed for services in 1877 with the dedication of St. Nathaniel. In 1885 the dedication was changed to St. Bartholomew on the insistence of the then Archbishop of York. The former sacristy was replaced by an iron church opened December 1891. This was demolished c.1941. The churchyard and cemetery were made into gardens by the corporation in 1959-60. They are now grassed over.

Interior of St. Bartholomew's Church, Hedon Road (141), c.1930. (B. Green).

142. HEDON ROAD. Primitive Methodist chapel. Built in 1894 at a cost of £1,100 with seating for 380. Designed by W.A. Gelder. Brick with Gothic detailing to doors and windows. It replaced a smaller building at the rear which had been built in 1877. Destroyed by bombing in 1941. Industrial building now on the site.

143. LEE SMITH STREET. Hedon Road Wesleyan chapel. A small Wesleyan mission room with seating for 150 was opened in Lee Smith Street in 1866. It was taken over by Lutherans in 1910 and used as a Swedish mission into the 1920s. It then became a Roman Catholic mission by 1929 and after alterations it was known as St. Francis's Church. Destroyed by bombing in 1941. The site is now occupied by an industrial building.

Primitive Methodist Chapel, Hedon Road (142), c.1900.

144. HEDON ROAD. Marfleet Wesleyan chapel. Built 1873, red brick with yellow-brick and stone dressings. Closed 1910. Survives as a workshop.

145. MARFLEET AVENUE. Wesleyan church. Built 1908. Demolished 1990. Not on map OS ref. TA 140298.

Former Marfleet Wesleyan Chapel (144), 1986.

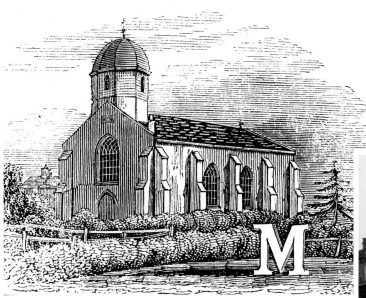

St. Giles, Marfleet (146),
(G. Poulson, History of Holderness, 1840).

Former Primitive Methodist Chapel, Sutton-on-Hull
(149), 1986.

146. MARFLEET. St. Giles's Anglican church. The first known mention of this church was c.1217, when it was a chapel-of-ease to the parish church of Paull in Holderness. In 1650 Marfleet was said to be 'fit to be made a parish', and in 1706 the church was described as a parish church. The medieval church building, no picture of which has yet been found, was completely rebuilt in 1793 to the design of George Pycock of Hull. The church was again completely rebuilt late in the 19th century to a design by J.T. Webster of Hedon and reopened in 1884. This building is still in use. Not on map OS ref. TA 143295.

147. SUTTON-ON-HULL. Wesleyan chapel, Church Street. Opened c.1812, rebuilt 1859. Incorporated into recreation club. Not on map OS ref. TA 116331.

148. SUTTON-ON-HULL. Primitive chapel, Chamberlain Street. Built 1832, rebuilt 1855, closed 1876 and demolished. Not on map OS ref. TA 117328.

149. SUTTON-ON-HULL. Primitive chapel, College Street. Built 1876 in Italianate style. Architect Joseph Wright. Closed 1933. Still standing. Not on map OS ref. TA 118328.

Appendix A - Pre-1920 purpose-built churches and chapels still standing 1991. Excluding Marfleet and Sutton.

(a) Those no longer in use as place of worship. Nos. refer to entries above.

Anlaby Rd., Salvation Army Ice House Citadel - empty. (47).

Anne St., Jewish Synagogue - nightclub. (22).

Courtney St., Baptist church - workshop/warehouse. (132).

Dagger Lane, Old Dagger Lane chapel - masonic hall. (2).

Dansom Lane, Wesleyan chapel - health centre. (131).

Hedon Rd., Marfleet Wesleyan chapel - workshop. (144).

Hessle Rd., Primitive Methodist chapel - derelict. (61).

Hodgson St., Primitive Methodist chapel - factory. (121).

Scott St., St. Gregory's RC school-chapel - workshop. (112).

Scott St., Wesleyan chapel - warehouse. (113).

Spring Bank, Swedenborgian church - secondhand furniture warehouse. (88).

Wilde St., Free Methodist chapel - warehouse. (130).

Wincolmlee, Primitive Methodist chapel - warehouse. (106).

Witham, Holborn St. chapel - office equipment store. (123).

(b) Those still in use as a place of worship.

Anlaby Rd., Plane St. Wesleyan chapel, school-chapel of 1895 on Plane St., church of 1910 facing Anlaby Rd., both by Gelder and Kitchen.

Beverley Rd., First Church of Christ Scientist. School built 1909, arch. M. Lenham; enlarged 1921; frontage 1923.

Beverley Rd., St. Anthony's Roman Catholic Convent, established by Sisters of Mercy, 1899, in an existing building. Additions were made in 1916, 1925 and 1931.

Beverley Rd., Trafalgar St. Baptist chapel, 1906 by G. Baines & Son of London. Earlier Baptist Tabernacle of 1892 adjoins in Trafalgar St. Now undenominational church.

Beverley Rd., Zion New Connexion Methodist chapel, Cave St., 1849. Now Glad Tidings Hall.

Boulevard, St. Matthew's Anglican church, 1870, archts: Adam and Kelly.

Clough Rd., St. John's Anglican church, Newland, consecrated 1833, arch: William Hutchinson, extensions and alterations 1893 and 1902, archts: Smith and Brodrick.

Franklin St., Salvation Army Citadel, built 1908.

Hawthorn Avenue, Salvation Army Citadel, built 1908.

Jarratt St., St. Charles Borromeo Roman Catholic church. Built 1828-9. Much altered 1894 by Smith, Brodrick and Lowther.

Lambert St., George Lamb Memorial Primitive Methodist chapel, 1894, by T.B. Thompson and W.A. Gelder.

Linnaeus St., Western synagogue, 1902, archt: B.S. Jacobs.

Lowgate, St. Mary's Anglican church, earliest known reference 1327.

Market Place, Holy Trinity Anglican church, earliest part of present building of c.1280.

Perth St., West St. Memorial Church, temporary building of 1908 survives as hall. New church 1931.

Prince's Avenue, Wesleyan Methodist church, 1905, archt. Gelder and Kitchen.

Prince's Avenue, Fish St. Memorial Congregational church, 1899, archt. W.H. Bingley. Now Elim Pentecostal City Temple.

Prince's Rd., Bethshan, 1903. Registered by the Independent Holiness Movement from 1958.

St. George's Rd., St. John the Baptist Anglican church, Newington, consecrated 1878, archts: Smith and Brodrick.

Sculcoates Lane, St. Mary's Anglican church, 1916, archt. Temple Moore.

Selby St., Primitive Methodist chapel, 1901, archt: T.B. Thompson, replaced earlier mission room of 1881 by Wm. Freeman.

Spring St., St. Patrick's Roman Catholic church. Built 1903-4.

Wheeler St., Wesleyan mission, 1900. Taken over by Churches of God c.1962.

Appendix B: Architects of Lost Churches and Chapels of Hull pre-1920.

Based on information supplied by Chris Ketchell and from K. J. Allison, ed., *Victoria County History, East Riding*, vol. 1, Hull, 1969, pp.293-333 and the unpublished Hull School of Architecture theses by B. W. Blanchard on 'Nonconformist Churches in the Hull District' (1955) and I. N. Goldthorpe on 'Architecture of the Victorian Era of Kingston upon Hull' (1955). Goldthorpe's thesis is soon to be published in a revised form by Humberside Libraries.

All the architects were based in Hull unless stated.

* Denotes the building was still standing October 1991.

(L) For further information see D. Linstrum, *West Yorkshire Architects and Architecture*, Lund Humphries, 1978

(N) For further information see Appendix B in D and S. Neave, *East Riding Chapels and Meeting Houses*, East Yorkshire Local History, 1990.

ADAMS, Richard L. (d.1883) and **John KELLY** (1840-1904) of Leeds. (L) Adams was architect of Leeds School Board from 1873. Kelly worked for three years in the office of G. E. Street. Partnership existed from c.1866-83. Architects of St. Andrew's Church, Holderness Road (1878) and also of St. Matthew's Church, Anlaby Road (1870)*.

ASTON, David Watson (fl.1851-68). Architect of St. Mary's RC school/chapel, Wilton St. (1855-6) and the chancel of St. Peter's, Drypool (1867).

ATKINSON, Thomas Beecroft (fl.1900-35). (N) Architect of Norman Memorial Primitive chapel, Hawthorn Avenue (1904-5).

BINGLEY, W. H. (fl.1890-1907). (N) Architect of Boulevard Free Methodist Church (1906-7) and Fish Street Memorial Congregational Church (now City Temple), Princes Avenue (1899)*.

BLESSLEY, Robert of London. Architect of St. Luke's Church, St. Luke Street (1862).

BOTTERILL, William (1820-1903). (N) An active Wesleyan. Established in Hull by 1851. Appointed architect to Hull School Board in 1873. By 1882 **John BILSON** (1856-1943) his former pupil had been taken into partnership and the firm became **Botterill, Son and Bilson**. Bilson took over the partnership in 1899. Architect of Newland Wesleyan Chapel, Cottingham Road (1858); Scott Street Wesleyan Chapel, alterations (1859)*; Beverley Road Wesleyan (1860-62); St. Mary, Sculcoates, alterations (1861-3); Carlton St. Wesleyan (1865); St. Nicolai Danish Church, Osborne St. (1870); Trinity Wesleyan Chapel, Coltman St. (1872); Wesleyan mission room, Lower Union St. (1882); St. Philip's Church, Charlotte St. (1885); St. Nicholas, Hessle Road (John Bilson) (1912).

BRODRICK, Cuthbert (1821-1905) (L). Hull's most celebrated Victorian architect did not design any of Hull's lost churches and chapels but he was responsible for the extension and remodelling of St. John's, Queen Victoria Square (1863).

DYKES, William Hey, junior, of Wakefield. Grandson of the Rev. Thomas Dykes the builder of St. John's. Architect of St. Paul's Church, St. Paul St. (1846).

FREEMAN, William (fl.1872-90) (N) Designed many Primitive chapels in Hull and East Riding. Architect of Lincoln St. Primitive (1872); St. George's Road (Beecroft Street) Primitive (1873 + 1889-90); Ebenezer Primitive, Spring Bank (1878); Hessle Road Primitive (1880)*; Selby Street Primitive (1881 + 1885); Campbell Street Free Methodist, alterations and additions (1882).

GELDER, Sir William Alfred, (1855-1941) (N). Born North Cave. In practice in Hull by 1877. Mayor of Hull five times (1899-1903). Active Wesleyan. Knighted 1903. Liberal MP for Brigg 1910-18. In partnership with **Llewellyn KITCHEN** as **GELDER and KITCHEN** from c.1898. Architect of Hodgson St. Primitive (1884)*; Brunswick Wesleyan Chapel, Holderness Road additions (1886); Presbyterian, Anlaby Road with T. B. Thompson (1891); St. John's Wesleyan, Stoneferry Rd. (1891); Lambert Street Primitive Chapel with T. B. Thompson (1893-4)*; Barnsley St. Wesleyan (1894); Hedon Rd. Primitive (1894); Plane St. Wesleyan school/chapel (1895)*; Argyle St. Wesleyan (1895); Groves Wesleyan, Jenning St. (1896); Newland Wesleyan school/chapel (1901); Bethesda Primitive, Holland St. (1902); St. George's Rd. Wesleyan, Hessle Rd. (enlarged 1904); Queen's Hall (Wesleyan), Alfred Gelder St. (1905); Portobello Street Primitive (1906); Thornton Hall (Wesleyan) Great Thornton St.

(1909); King's Hall (Wesleyan) Great Thornton St. (1909); King's Hall (Wesleyan), Fountain Rd. (1910); Barnsley St. Wesleyan extensions (1914).

GOLDIE, George (1828-1887) of London. Leading Roman Catholic architect. Designed Roman Catholic convent and school, Anlaby Rd. (1874).

GOUGH, Alexander Dick (1804-71) of London. Architect of a number of Anglican churches in London and south-east England. Architect of St. Andrew's Presbyterian Church, Prospect St. (1866).

HANSOM, Joseph Aloysius (1803-82) and **Edward WELCH** (1806-68) of York. (L) Hansom was inventor of the Hansom cab and founder of *The Builder*. Leading Roman Catholic architect. Architects of St. James, St. James Sq. (1831).

HILL, WILLIAM (1828-89) of Leeds. (L) Set up practice in Leeds in 1851. His firm is said to have been responsible for 'upwards of 100 Nonconformist chapels', many of them Methodist New Connexion. Architect of Stepney Methodist New Connexion, Beverley Rd. (1869).

HILLERNS, Oswald. Chartered engineer partner in O. Hillerns & Co., corn and seed merchants, High Street, Hull. Only known architectural work was German Lutheran Church, Nile St. (1910).

HUTCHINSON, William (1779-1869). Architect of Christ Church, Worship St. (1822) and St. Peter's Church, Drypool (1822-23). Also designed St. John's Church, Newland (1835)*.

JENKINS, William (b.1763) of London. Leading Wesleyan chapel architect. Designed Waltham St. Wesleyan (1814).

KERBY, William (fl.1862-65). Architect of chancel and vestry of Christ Church, Worship St. (1863), and the Protestant Institute, Kingston Sq. (1865). Also designed St. Peter's Church, Anlaby (1865).

KITCHING, William Henry (1840-1928). In practice in Hull by 1864. Architect of Campbell St. Free Methodist (1866); Wycliffe Congregational, Anlaby Rd. (1868); Presby-

terian, Holderness Rd. (1874); Wycliffe chapel spire (1875); Unitarian, Park St. (1881).

LOCKWOOD, Henry Francis (1811-78) (L) From Doncaster. Set up practice in Hull in 1834. Architect of Trinity House Chapel 1839-42. Became a partner of William Mawson in 1849 and they opened an office in Bradford where they soon became the leading firm. Architect of Albion St. Congregational (1842); Great Thornton Street Wesleyan (1842); St. Marks, St. Mark St. (1844); St. Stephens Church, St. Stephen's Sq. (1845).

MOORE, Temple Lushington (1856-1920) of London. Pupil then assistant to G.G. Scott, junr. Own practice from c.1882 onwards. Redesigned St. Augustine's, Queen's Rd. (1896).

MOULDS and PORRITT of Bury, Manchester and London. Architects of Newland Congregational, Beverley Rd. (1903).

MUSGRAVE, Samuel (fl.1870-85) (N) Architect and builder. A High Church Anglican who designed numerous nonconformist chapels as well as Anglican churches. Architect of St. Silas, Barmston St. (1871) (R.G. Smith won competition); Lincoln St. Primitive (1872); St. Barnabas, Hessle Rd. (1874); Latimer Congregational, Williamson St. (1874); Hessle Rd. Congregational (1875-6); Brunswick Wesleyan, Holderness Rd. (1877); Queen's Road Wesleyan (1878); All Saints', Margaret Street, tower (1883).

PETTINGELL, Frank Noble (1848-83). (N) Architect and water colour artist. Drew the well-known bird's eye view of Hull c.1880. Architect of Hodge Memorial Primitive, Williamson St. (1873).

PYCOCK, George (1749-99). Architect of St. Giles' church Marfleet (1793). Also designed Hull Infirmary (1783), and Neptune Inn (Boots), Whitefriargate (1794)*.

SCOTT, George Gilbert junior (1839-97) of London. Architect of St. Augustine's, Queen's Rd. (with T. L. Moore 1896).

SIMPSON, Edward (1844-1937) of Bradford (L). Son of a Hull builder, worked in London before settling in Bradford. He developed a large, almost exclusively Roman Catholic, practice. Architect of St. Jude's, Spring Bank (1874); St. Thomas's, Campbell St. (1882); St. Mary's Convent, Wilton/

Dansom St. (1900-1).

SIMPSON, James (1792-1864) of Leeds. (L) Leading Methodist Chapel architect particularly in West Riding. Architect of Kingston Wesleyan, Witham (1841).

SISSONS, William (fl.1833-76). Architect, surveyor and contractor. Architect of Wesley chapel, Humber St. (1833); Church Street Primitive, Wincolmlee (1846); 1849 Great Thornton Street Primitive (1849, rebuilt 1856); Clowes Primitive, Jarratt St. (1851).

SMITH, Richard George (fl.1861-98) and **Frederick Stead BRODRICK** (1847-1927) (N) Smith was in practice in Hull by 1861. By 1873 he was in partnership with Frederick Stead Brodrick, nephew of Cuthbert Brodrick. F.S. Brodrick succeeded his uncle as York Diocesan Surveyor in 1877. Smith and Brodrick was the leading architectural firm in Hull and the East Riding in later 19th century. It became Smith, Brodrick and Lowther then Brodrick, Lowther and Walker. In 1869 R.G. Smith won the competitions for St. Silas, Barmston Street (but designs provided by S. Musgrave) and for All Saints', Margaret Street (but commission awarded to G.E. Street). Smith and Brodrick were architects of Presbyterian, Spring Bank (1873-5); St. Paul's, St. Paul St. (1877); St. Luke's, St. Luke St. tower and spire (1881); St. Mark's, St. Mark St., alterations (1881). Also designed St. John the Baptist Church, Newington (1878)*.

Smith, Brodrick and **(Arthur) LOWTHER**, from c.1890, architects of St. Mary's R.C. Church, Wilton St. (1890-1); St. Bartholomew's, Hedon Rd. they supervised erection of iron church (1891-2); St. Gregory's R.C. church/school, Scott St. (1893)*; St. Wilfrid's R.C., Boulevard (1895-6).

Brodrick, Lowther and **(William Snowball) WALKER** by 1900. Architects of St. Mary and St. Peter, Hessle Rd. (1902) (W.S. Walker); St. Saviour's, Stoneferry Rd. (1903); Church of Transfiguration, Albert Avenue (1904) (F.S. Brodrick).

STREET, George Edmund (1824-81) of London. Leading Victorian church architect. For his work in East Yorkshire see J. Hutchinson and P. Joyce, *George Edmund Street in East Yorkshire*, University of Hull, 1981. Architect of All Saints',

Margaret Street (1869).

THOMPSON, T. Brownlow (d.1929) (N) Established in Hull by 1876. A Presbyterian. Architect of St. George's Rd. Wesleyan, Hessle Rd. (1877 + 1883); Presbyterian, Anlaby Road (1891-3) (with W.A. Gelder); Selby Street Primitive (1901)*; Boulevard Baptist, Gordon Street (1903) (with John F. Fisher). Also architect of Lambert St. Primitive (1893-4)* with W.A. Gelder.

WALTERS, Frederick Arthur (1850-1932). Leading Roman Catholic architect. Pupil of George Goldie. Architect for rebuilding of Buckfast Abbey. Designed French Convent, Park Grove (1914-15).

WRIGHT, Joseph (1818-1885) (N). Pupil of Cuthbert Brodrick. An active Primitive Methodist and architect of many chapels in East Yorkshire and North Lincolnshire. Architect of Bright St. Primitive Chapel, Holderness Rd. (1864); Jubilee Primitive, Spring Bank (1864); Emmanuel Primitive, Stoneferry Rd. (1870); Bourne Primitive, Anlaby Rd. (1871); Sutton-on-Hull Primitive (1876)*; Zion Primitive, Fountain Rd. (1877).

INDEX BY STREET

Nos. in brackets refer to note on each church or chapel in gazetteer.

*signifies illustration.

Abbreviations used: Bapt - Baptist; CoE - Church of England; Cong. - Congregational; Ind. - Independent; NCM - New Connexion Methodist; Pres. - Presbyterian; Prim. - Primitive; RC - Roman Catholic; Sw. - Swedenborgian; Wes. - Wesleyan.

New George St. Prim. (114).

Nile St. Cong./Bapt./Prim./CoE/German Lutheran (46)*.

North St. (later Charlotte St.) Bethel NCM (42)*.

North St. (off Prospect St.) RC (27)*.

Osborne St. Bapt./Ind. Meth. (21)*; Bethesda Cong./Danish Lutheran (43)*; Synagogue (Anne St.) (22)*.

Oxford St. Wes. (110).

Parade Row Synagogue (20).

Paragon St. Christian Temperance/Bapt. (25)*.

Park Grove Convent RC (95).

Park St. Unitarian (85)*.

Porter St. Cong./Wes./CoE/Ind. (52).

Portobello St. Prim. (140)*.

Posterngate RC/Jew (3)*, Mariners' Church (4).

Prospect St. St. Andrew's Free CoE/Presb. (31)*.

Queen's Dock Floating Chapel (17)*.

Queen's Rd. St. Augustine's CoE (98)*.

Queen Victoria Sq. St. John the Evangelist CoE (19)*.

Raikes St., Drypool Wes. (116).

Robinson Row Synagogue (5).

St. George's Rd. Beecroft St. Prim. (68)*.

St. James's Square St. James's CoE (55)*.

St. Luke's St. St. Luke's CoE (49)*.

St. Mark's Sq. Wes. (58).

St. Mark's St. St. Mark's CoE (120)*.

St. Paul's St. St. Clement's CoE (105)*; St. Paul's CoE (111)*.

St. Stephen's Sq. St. Stephen's CoE (84)*.

Salthouse Lane Bapt. (14).

School St. Synagogue (33).

Scott St. St. Gregory's RC (112)*; Wes. (113)*.

South St. Bapt. (24)*.

Spring Bank St. Jude's CoE (90)*; Ebenezer Prim. (91)*; Jubilee Prim. (87)*; Pres. (86)*; Sw. (88)*.

Stoneferry Rd. St. Saviour's CoE (133)*; Bethel Wes. (135); Emmanuel Prim. (134); St. John's Wes. (136)*.

Sutton on Hull Wes. (147); Prim. (148/149*).

Sykes St. Tabernacle Cong./Wes./Pres./Prim. (38)*.

Walker St. Zion Wes. Reformers/Cong. (50).

Waltham St. Wes. (34)*.

Walton St. Pres. (77).

West Parade (Spring Bank) Wes. (89).

Westmorland St. Salvation Army (107).

Wilde St. Free Meth. (130)*.

Williamson St. Prim. (128)*; Latimer Cong. (127)*.

Wilton St. St. Mary's RC (124)*.

Wincolmlee Church St. Prim. (106)*.

Witham Holborn St. Cong./Prim. (123)*; Kingston Wes. (122)*.

Worship Street Christ Church CoE (37)*.

DENOMINATIONAL INDEX. Nos. refer to note in gazetteer.

Anglican churches: All Sts. 94; Christ Church 37; Mariners' Church 4,6; St. Andrew 129; St. Augustine 98; St. Barnabas 63; St. Bartholomew 141; St. Clement 105; St. Giles, Marfleet 146; St. James 55; St. John the Evangelist 19; St. Jude 90; St. Luke 49; St. Mark 120; St. Mary, Sculcoates 102; St. Mary & St. Peter 71; St. Nicholas 72; St. Paul 111; St. Peter, Drypool 115; St. Philip 41; St. Saviour 133; St. Silas 108; St. Stephen 84; St. Thomas 81; Transfiguration 74.

Nonconformist and other places of worship:

Baptist 6, 10, 14, 18, 21, 24, 25, 35, 40, 46, 66, 132; Christian Temperance 25; Congregational/Independent 2, 6, 7, 8, 12, 23, 26, 32, 38, 43, 46, 50, 51, 52, 62, 83, 99, 123, 127; Free Church of England 30, 31; Free Methodist 26, 38, 64, 82, 130; Independent Methodist 21, 44, 50; Jewish 3, 5, 20, 22, 33, 44, 51; Lutheran Danish 43, German 46; Methodist New Connexion 21, 24, 38, 42, 96; Presbyterian 1, 2, 11, 31, 38, 76, 77, 86, 125; Primitive Methodist 24, 29, 36, 38, 39, 40, 46, 54, 59, 61, 68, 70, 73, 78, 87, 91, 104, 106, 109, 114, 121, 126, 128, 134, 139, 140, 142, 148, 149; Quaker 13, 39; Roman Catholic 3, 27, 28, 65, 80, 95, 112, 124, 143; Salvation Army 47, 48, 60, 106, 107; Swedenborgian 2, 88; Unitarian 11, 18, 85; Wesleyan Association 38, 40; Wesleyan Methodist 9, 10, 15, 16, 26, 34, 38, 39, 44, 45, 53, 56, 57, 58, 67, 69, 75, 79, 89, 92, 93, 97, 100, 101, 103, 110, 113, 116, 117, 118, 119, 122, 131, 135, 136, 137, 138, 143, 144, 145, 147; Wesleyan Reformers 24, 38, 50, 52.